Frommer's®

24 GREAT walks in PARIS

2nd Edition

WILEY

Wiley Publishing, Inc.

Authors: Peter and Oriel Caine
Series Editor: Donna Wood
Art Editor: Alison Fenton
Copy Editor: Felicity Jackson
Proofreader: Polly Boyd
Picture Researcher: Michelle Aylott
Cartography provided by the Mapping Services
Department of AA Publishing
Production: Stephanie Allen

Edited, designed and produced by AA Publishing.
© AA Media Limited 2010
This edition revised and updated June 2010

All rights reserved. No part of this publication may be
reproduced, stored in a retrieval system, or transmitted
in any form or by any means – electronic, photocopying,
recording or otherwise – unless the written permission of
the publishers has been obtained beforehand. This book
may not be lent, resold, hired out or otherwise disposed
of by way of trade in any form of binding other than that
in which it is published, without the prior consent of the
publisher.

Published by AA Publishing.

Published in the United States by
Wiley Publishing, Inc.
111 River Street, Hoboken, NJ 07030

Find us online at Frommers.com

Frommer's is a registered trademark of Arthur Frommer.
Used under license.

Mapping in this title produced from:
Paris data © Tele Atlas N.V. 2010 **Tele Atlas**
France: © IGN France.

ISBN 978-0-470-92817-2

A04510

A CIP catalogue record for this book is available from the
British Library.

The contents of this publication are believed correct
at the time of printing. Nevertheless, the publishers
cannot accept responsibility for errors or omissions,
or for changes in details given in this guide or for
the consequences of any reliance on the information
provided by the same. Assessments of attractions and
so forth are based upon the author's own experience
and, therefore, descriptions given in this guide necessarily
contain an element of subjective opinion which may not
reflect the publishers' opinion or dictate a reader's own
experiences on another occasion.

Printed in China by Leo Paper Group

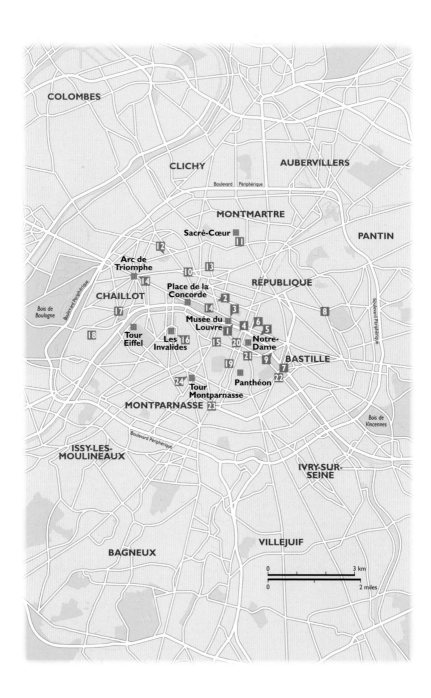

COLOMBES

CLICHY

AUBERVILLERS

PANTIN

MONTMARTRE

Sacré-Cœur **11**

12

Arc de
Triomphe
14

10

13

RÉPUBLIQUE

CHAILLOT

Place de la
Concorde

2

3

8

Bois de
Boulogne

17

14

Musée du
Louvre

1

4

6

5

Bois de
Vincennes

18

Tour
Eiffel

Les
Invalides

16

15

20

Notre-
Dame

21

9

BASTILLE

7

22

19

Panthéon

24

Tour
Montparnasse

23

MONTPARNASSE

ISSY-LES-
MOULINEAUX

IVRY-SUR-
SEINE

BAGNEUX

VILLEJUIF

0   3 km
0   2 miles

CONTENTS

Introduction 6

1   The Birthplace of the City   8
2   Pyramids and Palaces   14
3   The French Paradox   22
4   Alchemists and Artists   28
5   Knights and Mansions   36
6   Saints and Sinners   42
7   Backstreets of the Bastille   50
8   Home of the Famous Dead   56
9   The Romantic Island   64
10   The Madeleine District   72
11   Bohemian Montmartre   78
12   How the Other Half Live   84
13   The Phantom of the Opera   92
14   The Golden Triangle   98
15   The Bridges of Paris   106
16   Glorifying the Military   112
17   The Iron Lady of Paris   120
18   Art Nouveau to Art Deco   126
19   Following the Rose Line   134
20   From Romans to the Revolution   140
21   Down and Out in Paris   148
22   Old-World Forgotten Paris   154
23   Down Among the Bones   162
24   Painters' Paris   168
    Index   174
    Acknowledgements   176

Introduction

Parisians call their home 'the city of a hundred villages' because each district has a distinct personality and character, as well as its own portion of history and mystery. This book explores 24 different quartiers (districts) of Paris, introducing you to the city's most famous monuments, but also leading you to some quiet, ancient or tucked-away curios that even native Parisians may not be aware of.

There is an introduction to each walk, which touches on the general history of the area, giving you a flavour of what is to come when you start walking. Paris is the capital of culinary delights and, as there is nothing like a stroll to whet your appetite, each walk includes recommendations for some of the best places to stop for lunch, coffee, a pastry or snacks.

If you are visiting Paris for the first time, then Île de la Cité (Walk 1), the Marais (Walks 5 and 6), the Latin quarter (Walk 20), and Montmartre (Walk 11) are essential tours. If you wish to follow a chronological history of Paris, then start with Walk 1, The Birthplace of the City. Go on to Walks 19 and 20 in the Latin quarter, then Walk 3 in Les Halles. In so doing, you will follow the development of the city, which began on the Île de la Cité in the pre-Roman era, then spread to the Left Bank, and over to the Right Bank in medieval times.

The Renaissance period is visited on Walks 5 and 6 in the lovely Marais quarter. Traces of the French Revolution are encountered on many of the walks, but particularly in the unusual and atmospheric Les Catacombes (Walk 23). In 19th-century Paris, widespread urban development took place. Between 1850 and 1870 Paris doubled in size, the old city centre was 70 percent demolished and then rebuilt under the control of Baron Haussmann. This city of avenues and boulevards can be seen on Walk 13, 'The Phantom of the Opera', and Walk 12, 'How the Other Half Live'. The latter walk takes you to visit the magnificent mansions of the

19th-century Monceau district. Having completed these walks, follow up with a visit to the Musée Carnavalet, where you can journey through the history of Paris. The museum is free.

Do not leave Paris without visiting the magical Montmartre quarter (Walk 11). This walk takes about two and a half hours but, factoring in the magnificent views across Paris from the top of the hill, the bustling artists' square and tempting restaurants, you can easily spend half a day there.

All the walks are between 1.2 and 2.4 miles (2 and 4km) long and, except Montmartre, are relatively flat. Suggested times have been included, but how long you spend on each walk obviously depends on how you pace yourself, and how often you stop.

It is well worth purchasing the 2, 4, or 6-day museum pass, which gets you into museums avoiding the queues. Don't forget to ask for the booklet that lists participating museums when you buy the pass. This is available at the Paris Tourist Office, 25 rue des Pyramides, www.parismuseumpass.fr. The pass can be bought online at the above address before you even leave home. Most museums are free for under-18s, some offer reduced rates for 18–25 year olds, and most are closed on Mondays or Tuesdays.

Paris is lovely at any time of year, but walking is never better than in spring or autumn. The month of August is the principal French holiday period; at this time of year Parisians flock to the countryside, leaving Paris to go into a sleepy hibernation. Although it can be very hot in August, it is one of the best times for visitors. Remember to wear comfortable walking shoes, and consider wearing a hat in summer. Always carry a small bottle of water. During the hottest part of the day you may want to take refuge in cool church interiors or in one of the city's shady parks.

Enjoy the walks in this guide and don't be afraid to add to your pleasure by pushing doorways open in order to discover your own 'secret Paris'.

The Birthplace of the City

Trace the origins of Paris, an ancient citadel that began as an island. Here on the Île de la Cité, every period of history has left its mark.

Archaeological evidence suggests that a Celtic tribe called the Parisii first settled on the Île de la Cité island in the middle of the River Seine during the 3rd century BC. Île de la Cité was a secure settlement, having the Seine as a natural moat, but no defence was sufficient to protect the Celts from Roman invasion in 52BC. There was relative peace between Romans and Celts, and the city, renamed Lutetia (meaning born of the waters), prospered. The Parisii had been boat builders and competent sailors, inspiring Roman administrators to choose the ship as their symbol. The Latin motto for Paris became *Fluctuat Nec Mergitor,* meaning 'Paris the unsinkable ship'. The emblem and motto are still used today. In the Roman period the island was divided by a north/south axis: the east was residential and the centre of spiritual life, the west was administrative. Today the same divide exists, but the medieval cathedral Notre-Dame replaces the Roman temple to Jupiter. In the 19th century, many churches and the maze of medieval houses were demolished and the long straight streets of Haussmann were built. The modern Mémorial de la Déportation (Monument to the Deported) brings the island up to date, so that 2,000 years of history can be traced here.

| Leave Pont Neuf Métro station and cross the bridge, admiring the magnificent views. Stop halfway, at the statue.

Pont Neuf means New Bridge, but, ironically, it is the oldest in Paris and was the first to be built of stone and to be free of houses. The semicircular side bays were originally market stalls used by teeth-pullers, quack doctors and other merchants. The original statue of Henry IV was melted down during the Revolution. The anti-Royalist who replaced it secretly hid a statuette of Napoleon in the horse's belly; this was recently discovered during restoration work. Steps beside the statue lead down to the square du Vert Galant, where Jacques de Molay, Grand Master of the Templars, was burnt at the stake, cursing the kings as he was consumed by the flames. La Samaritaine department store on the Right Bank has an imposing art deco façade. Its founder left his collection of furniture to the city of Paris; it is now in the Musée Cognacq-Jay.

2 From the statue, cross the road into place Dauphine and turn left into rue de Harlay, walking around the Conciergerie. Turn right into boulevard du Palais, cross over to place Louis Lépine, stopping to admire the Conciergerie and the Sainte-Chapelle.

The Conciergerie was the royal palace before the Louvre was built. During the Revolution it became a prison where some 2,600 prisoners were kept before being guillotined. Marie Antoinette's cell can be visited and the building is now the Museum of the Revolution. The westernmost tower facing the Seine is where prisoners were tortured. Since their screams could be heard across the river, it is called the Tour Bon Bec, meaning 'Big Mouth Tower'. A combined ticket can be purchased for visiting both the museum and the Sainte-Chapelle, built in the 1240s. The stained glass windows here are the finest in Paris, being intended for the private chapel of the King. St Louis had the chapel built to house the Crown of Thorns and other precious holy relics that can now be seen in Notre-Dame.

CONCIERGERIE;

DAILY 9.30–6; www.monum.fr

WHERE TO EAT

|O| PANIS,
21 Quai de Montbello;
Tel: 01 43 54 19 71.
Traditional brasserie. Copious portions in a lovely location.

|O| LA RESERVE DE QUASIMODO,
4 rue de la Colombe;
Tel: 01 46 34 67 67.
Restaurant and wine tasting, very picturesque in historic setting.

|O| LE GRENIER DE NOTRE-DAME,
18 rue de la Bucherie;
Tel: 01 43 29 98 29.
Vegetarian food served in an attractive setting.

DISTANCE 1.5 miles (2.5km)

ALLOW 2 hours

START Pont Neuf Métro station

FINISH Hôtel de Ville Métro station

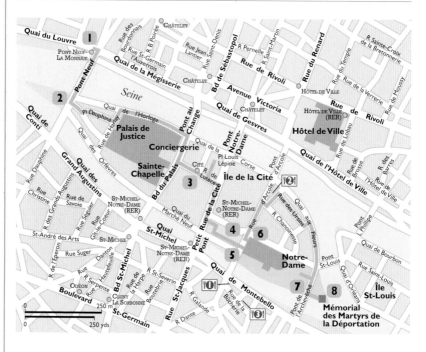

3 Walk along rue de Lutèce; the colourful flower market is on the left. Turn right into rue de la Cité, then left onto the place du Parvis, in front of Notre-Dame.

The 19th-century hospital, Hôtel Dieu, is on the left side of the square (place du Parvis) and its interior courtyard and gardens can be visited. This building replaced the medieval hospital that was

run by the cathedral. In medieval times there were three people per bed – one sick, one dying and one dead. The original hospital buildings were on the Pont au Double, linking the island to the Left Bank. Beneath the square is the Crypte Archaeologique, where remains of Gallo Roman houses can be seen alongside the foundations of ancient buildings, a medieval road and part of Paris's 3rd-century city wall.

4 Pause to admire the façade of the cathedral.

A brass stud in the pavement in front of the cathedral marks the Zero Point of Paris. This has become a 'Wishing Stone' but is actually the point from which distances to other towns are measured. The first stone of the cathedral was laid at the rear end in 1163, and the builders finished with the façade in the 1220s, having spent some 60 years at work. Notre-Dame means 'Our Lady' or the Virgin Mary. She is shown as a child with her mother, St Anne, above the right-hand portal; the death of the Virgin is represented on the left portal. Above the main entrance the sculptures represent Judgement Day with St Michael weighing souls, and a devil leading the damned towards the gates of hell. The curious figure in a round medallion at the foot of Christ on the central column is an allegory of Alchemy; the ladder of nine steps symbolizes the path to attaining the secret knowledge. The row of 27 huge figures beneath the rose window represents the biblical kings who are the ancestors of Christ. These statues are copies, because the originals, mistaken for French kings during the Revolution, were destroyed. The Emanuel bell hangs in the left tower but has not been rung since the Liberation of Paris as its vibration causes structural damage.

5 Enter Notre-Dame through the right-hand portal.

Immediately inside the door you are beneath the bell tower. Look up at the vault to see the trapdoor through which the bells were hoisted. The two pillars that support the weight of the towers are massive. The cathedral itself is huge and can accommodate a congregation of 9,000. The only original 13th-century glass can be seen in the three rose windows. The façade rose is partially obscured by the organ, which is the largest in France, with 7,500 pipes, 110 stops and 5 keyboards. At the rear end, to the right, is the Treasury containing what is purported to be the Crown of Thorns. At the very back, in a side chapel, is a series of models that show how the medieval builders constructed the cathedral. The 14th-century carved screen around the altar shows easily recognizable bible stories. The white marble Pietà at the main altar stands between statues of Louis XIII and his son Louis XIV.

NOTRE-DAME; DAILY 8.00–6.45;

TEL: 01 42 34 56 10; www.monum.fr

6 Leave the church by the north portal and turn right along rue d'Arcole, then right into rue Chanoinesse. Take the first left into picturesque rue de la Colombe, then turn right into rue des Ursins. Go up the steps on your left to the quai aux Fleurs and walk along the quai until you come to square Jean XXIII behind Notre-Dame.

The views from the garden are superb. Stop to admire the Seine, the cathedral spire and its magnificent flying buttresses. These buttresses enabled the builders to achieve great height because they carry the weight of the stone-vaulted roof. The walls could be pierced with large bays containing stained glass because they were no longer needed for support. Before the discovery of this technique in the 13th century, large windows could not be used. The buttresses have gutters along their backs, which channel rainwater into the mouths of the gargoyles, made famous by the author Victor Hugo in his novel *The Hunchback of Notre-Dame* and the subsequent film starring Charles Laughton as the hunchback, Quasimodo. Hugo's novel appeared at a time when Gothic architecture was not popular. Its success initiated restoration of the cathedral.

7 Cross quai de l'Archèveché to leave the garden. Walk into the square de l'Île de France at the east end of the island. Go down steps into Le Mémorial des Martyrs de la Déportation.

This underground memorial is dedicated to the 200,000 people deported from France by the Nazis during World War II who later died in concentration camps. A corridor is studded with 200,000 glass pearls, one for each person. The black marble tomb in the foreground is that of an unknown deportee, symbolizing all. On either side of the memorial are concrete chambers that re-create the concentration camp cells. An eternal flame is kept burning. The inscription reads 'Forgive – but do not forget.'

8 End the walk here or carry on with Walk 9 by crossing the Pont St-Louis to the Île St-Louis. The nearest Métro station, Hôtel de Ville, is at the far end of Pont d'Arcole.

13

Pyramids and Palaces

For centuries the site of the French court, the Musée du Louvre dominates this district, but there are plenty of lesser-known attractions.

The Louvre was built in the 12th century, but subsequent epochs added a wing or modified it, resulting in a palace of 8 miles (12.8km) of corridors. The latest major change took place in the last years of Mitterrand's presidency, when the architect I. M. Pei was commissioned to build the stunning glass pyramid and convert the northern side of the building from offices of the old Finance Ministry into museum galleries. The pyramid earned President Mitterrand the nickname 'the Sphinx'. After several years of work, the pyramid opened in 1989, to coincide with the bicentenary of the French Revolution. The Richelieu Wing opened in 1994, to celebrate the 200th anniversary of the museum. The royal collections opened to the public at the end of the Revolution in 1794. Next to the Louvre stands the Palais Royale, which was once home to Cardinal Richelieu. Comedie Française and the Ministry of Culture now occupy the buildings. This circuit will take you into a lovely quiet garden where you can enjoy a picnic lunch. The arcades at the end are great for a spot of shopping.

1 As you leave Pyramides Métro station, look along avenue de l'Opéra for the view, then walk down rue des Pyramides. Pass the Paris Tourist Office at No. 25, turn right into rue St-Honoré and go into the church of St-Roch on your right.

Built in the 17th and 18th centuries, this beautiful church is dedicated to the patron of plague victims. He is always shown indicating a wound on his leg, and with his companion, a dog who brought him sustenance. Go right to the back of the church and you will see a delightful sculpture of Mary and Joseph, who are looking in surprise and wonderment at the baby Jesus.

2 Leaving the church, turn left and return to rue des Pyramides. Turn right and stop at the gilded statue of Joan of Arc on horseback, created by the sculptor Frémiet (1824-1910).

St Joan was wounded here in 1426 trying to take Paris from the English during the Hundred Years War. The city walls of the time were very near here.

3 Turn right into rue de Rivoli, cross the road at the pedestrian crossing and enter the Jardin des Tuileries. Cross into the central axis in order to admire the view of the obelisk and the Arc de Triomphe in the distance.

The Tuileries Gardens were designed in 1664 by Le Notre, gardener to Louis XIV. Comprising well-manicured lawns,

WHERE TO EAT

🍴 A PRIORI THÉ,
35-37 Galerie Vivienne;
Tel: 01 42 97 48 75.
Pretty tearoom, good for snacks.

🍴 LE NEMOURS,
2 Galerie Nemours, Place Colette;
Tel: 01 42 61 34 14.
Light lunches outdoors under the arcades.

🍴 BAR RESTAURANT 'LES VARIÉTÉS',
12 passage des Panoramas;
Tel: 01 42 36 98 09.
Charming old-fashioned bistro.

flowerbeds and spectacular statuary, they stretch from the Louvre to Concorde Square and provide a welcome resting place away from the traffic-choked streets. The gardens are reputed to be haunted at night by the bloodstained spectre of one of Catherine de Medici's victims (Medici once lived in the Tuileries Palace).

4 Turn and walk in the opposite direction, past large bronze sculptures by Maillol (1861-1944), and continue to the Place du Carrousel.

The arch was ordered by Napoleon as the gateway to his palace, which once stood here overlooking the Tuileries Gardens. He then wanted a larger arch, which was ultimately to be the Arc de Triomphe. When the Tuileries Palace burned down

15

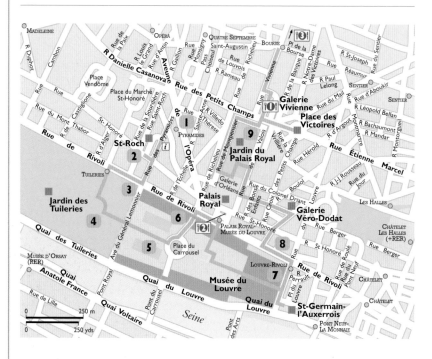2

DISTANCE 2.5 miles (4km)

ALLOW 3 hours

START Pyramides Métro station

FINISH Bourse Métro station

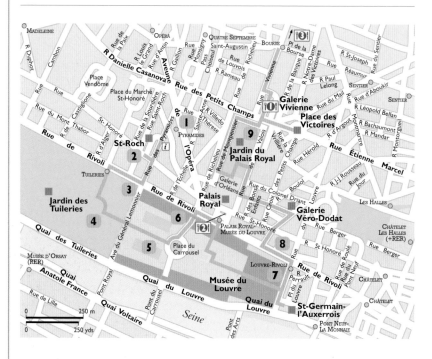

in 1871, the two arches could be seen together for the first time, as the palace no longer blocked the view. On the top of the Arc de Carrousel Napoleon placed the four horses from St Mark's in Venice, which he had requisitioned. They had to be replaced by copies when the Venetians asked for them back.

5 As you face the pyramid, go down the steps to the right of the arch, taking the underground access to the Louvre. If you wish to visit the museum,

use this entrance. At the bottom of the steps are the old city walls.

Ahead is the inverted glass pyramid and the smaller upright stone one, famous as the resting place of the Holy Grail in Dan Brown's *The Da Vinci Code*. There is a variety of shops here, toilets, a lively food hall, and a tourist office. If you do not wish to visit the museum but want to see the glass pyramid from inside, go through the security check and walk straight on. You can have a coffee under the pyramid.

OPPOSITE: JARDIN DES TUILERIES

The view is superb from inside, as you look through the pyramid at the elaborate architecture of the Louvre. Dan Brown claimed that it consists of 666 panes of glass – the number symbolizing the devil. **LOUVRE;** MON, THU, SAT–SUN 9–6, WED & FRI 9–10. 1ST SUN OF MONTH FREE; www.louvre.fr

6 From the inverted pyramid, walk out of the shopping mall and go up the steps to the exit, turn right into rue de Rivoli, and continue until you find the entrance on the right leading through to the pyramid. As you walk through, look into the Musée du Louvre through the glass walls on the left. Go round the pyramid on the left, past the brass studs in the paving, which mark the Rose Line of *The Da Vinci Code*. Go into the large courtyard on the left.

The Louvre was once the palace of the kings of France and various rulers added different wings over the ages. Look at the sides of the courtyard and identify the kings and queens by their initials. H is for Henry II, interlaced with C for his wife Catherine, L is for Louis XIII, interlaced with A for his wife Anne of Austria, and LB is for Louis de Bourbon. A rooster, the symbol of France, stands in the pediment above one of the exit arches. Walk to the middle of the square and look to the right through the arch for a beautiful view of the Institute of France on the far side of the river.

7 Leave by the exit opposite the one by which you entered. Ahead you can see, to the left, the town hall of the first arrondissement; in the centre, the bell tower with its famous carillon bells; also in the centre, and on the right, the church of St-Germain-l'Auxerrois, built between the 13th and 16th centuries. Cross the road and enter the church.

Once the royal church, it was used by the kings when they were in residence at the Louvre. It has a superb example of a Renaissance painted altarpiece on the right-hand side towards the back. It illustrates the story of Mary, her mother Saint Anne, and various apocryphal stories associated with them. Look at the scene of Mary's birth, noticing how the artist has put in homely details such as the bedroom with its fireplace, and the servants going about their tasks. During the religious wars, the signal was given for the terrible massacre of St Bartholomew from the bell tower of this church. On that day, in 1572, unarmed Protestants who had gathered to celebrate the marriage of the future Henry IV and Queen Margot were brutally murdered by the Catholics. The original bell tower, where the fatal bell was tolled, is at the back of the church.

8 Exit the church, pausing to look at the sculptures in the portal, then turn right and go ahead to rue de Rivoli. Turn left, and walk past a statue of Coligny, the Protestant leader. The massacre of St Bartholomew had been orchestrated to draw attention from an attempt to assassinate Coligny. Turn right along rue de Marengo, then right into rue Jean-Jacques Rousseau. Turn left into the pretty gallery Véro-Dodat, then go straight ahead until you come to the Palais Royal.

The palace was built for Cardinal Richelieu but was also lived in by members of the royal family (Louis XIV spent his childhood here). It now houses the Ministry of Culture. The black-and-white columns are a modern installation by abstract minimalist artist Daniel Buren (b.1938). They were once controversial but are now a popular attraction. Go into the main garden with its elegant frame of classical architecture, which is a delightful haven in the centre of the city. There is seating, a children's play area, a fountain, statues and flowerbeds. On either side, under the arcades, are specialist shops (tin soldiers, vintage clothes, musical boxes), cafés and restaurants.

9 Leave via an archway at the far end of the garden. Go right through another passageway, cross rue des Petits Champs and look right towards the statue of Louis XIV on his horse in the centre of place des Victoires. (You could make a detour to see this elegant royal square.) Continue through a charming arcade (Galerie Vivienne), enjoy the shops and perhaps stop at the tearoom, then turn right as you exit at the far end and walk along to Bourse Métro station.

GALERIE VIVIENNE

The French Paradox

Covered markets or 'halls' made Les Halles famous. The market's gone but this walk is still a gourmet's treat, taking in the finest French specialities.

Les Halles quarter takes its name from the covered markets that stood here until February 1969. There had been a market here for nearly 800 years, then Pompidou's government decided to demolish the old quarter and move the congested market place outside the city. The old market was famously described by Zola as 'the belly of Paris' and was a centralized distribution point for fresh produce in France, aimed specifically at the catering trade. The market ran till late at night so that chefs could come and purchase everything from pots and pans, and chef's uniforms, to raw ingredients. Despite the disappearance of the market, the old atmosphere can still be found in some of its streets, and several wholesalers remain. You will no longer hear the street cries of the vendors, but you can still buy a saucepan big enough to bathe in. Several curious monuments have survived the re-development, including Catherine de Medici's astrology column, the lovely church of St-Eustache and the Bourse de Commerce. The French paradox is of course the often-asked question: 'Just how do the French eat so much rich food and drink so much wine without putting on weight?'

I Start at Louvre-Rivoli Métro station and cross rue de Rivoli into rue J. Tison. Turn immediately right into rue Bailleul then left along rue de l'Arbre Sec and stop on the corner, at the junction with rue St-Honoré.

The fountain on the corner was built in 1776. The street name l'Arbre Sec means 'withered tree', and refers to the gibbet that once stood here; the small rooms above the fountain tower were built so that Parisian aldermen could get a good view of the executions. At No. 115 rue St-Honoré is a lovely 18th-century apothecary where Marie Antoinette's lover, Axel Fersen, used to buy invisible ink, which he used to write secret messages to the imprisoned queen.

2 Walk along rue Sauval until rue Berger. Stop to admire the tower directly ahead, then walk left along rue Berger, turn right into rue du Louvre and enter La Bourse du Commerce.

The large circular building of La Bourse was the Commodities Exchange for the old market. The curious tower was used as an observatory by the astrologer Ruggieri, who worked for the superstitious Catherine de Medici. Nostradamus had accurately predicted her husband's death and Ruggieri foretold the death of the queen. The present building dates from 1889. The interior ceiling is a magnificent painted dome showing trading scenes from around the world. Russia is represented by ships locked in snow and ice, Europe

WHERE TO EAT

🍴 AU PIED DE COCHON,
6 rue Coquillere;
Tel: 01 40 13 77 00.
Onion soup/traditional brasserie fare.

🍴 GALOPIN,
40 rue Notre-Dame des Victoires;
Tel: 01 42 36 45 38.
Traditional French cuisine in a lovely old interior.

🍴 STOHRER,
51 rue Montorgeuil;
Tel: 01 42 33 38 20.
The oldest patisserie in Paris.

by an idealized antique port, Asia and Africa by their indigenous populations in traditional attire, and the Americas by Native Americans with a steam train in the background. As you leave the central rotunda, note the clock and barometer above the door, which enabled accredited brokers to see whether their trade ships were making timely progress.

BOURSE DE COMMERCE;
MON–FRI 9–5; www.euronext.com

3 Leave the Bourse, turn right into rue du Louvre, then right again into rue Coquillère.

At No. 18 is Dehillerin – wholesale suppliers to the catering trade. Staff here speak perfect English, and you are more than welcome to go in and browse in this

OPPOSITE: STOHRER PATISSERIE

23

DISTANCE 1.5 miles (2.5km)

ALLOW 2–3 hours

START Louvre-Rivoli Métro station

FINISH Grands Boulevards Métro station

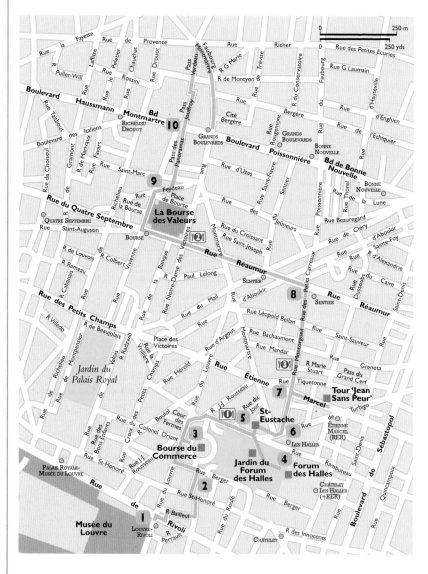

Aladdin's cave of kitchen paraphernalia. Among the treasures available here are the celebrated Peugeot brothers' pepper grinders - no other grinder is said to last as long or grind your pepper so perfectly. At No. 6 is the famous restaurant 'Au Pied de Cochon', which is permitted to stay open 24 hours a day as it once did to provide cheap and fortifying onion soup to the army of market porters. As its name suggests, one of its specialities is pigs' trotters. If you are not sure what this dish looks like, then take a close look at the restaurant's door handles.

4 **Walk across the gardens to the Forum des Halles, where a viewing stage gives a panorama over the underground shopping centre that replaced the old market.**

The original market halls, built in the mid-19th century, were light structures of iron and glass. They became the prototype for covered markets all around France. Originally, 10 pavilions, each divided into 250 stalls, covered the garden area and shopping centre, now called the Forum. The market became a veritable institution, the beating heart of Paris. Those who remember it as it was lament the loss of the atmosphere of the hard-working culinary vendors and their soulful cries, the bistros serving onion soup, and the porters, prostitutes and other colourful figures for which the area was famous. This atmosphere was marvellously captured in the film *Irma La Douce,* starring Jack Lemmon and Shirley MacLaine. Parisians were shocked

when they learnt of Pompidou's plans to redevelop the area. The government assured the public that nothing could be done to save the market and eventually it closed, in February 1969. In 1971 Parisians stood by and watched the ancient heart of their city being torn out. The modern-day shopping centre was inaugurated in 1979 and is of little interest with the exception of the huge supermarket, the FNAC. Its green garden trellises are intended to evoke the lost pavilions of the original market.

5 **Leave the gardens and enter the church of St-Eustache.**

This huge church is indicative of the wealth generated by the market and the close proximity of the one-time Royal Palace, the Louvre. It is rich in aristocratic associations: Richelieu, Molière and Madame de Pompadour were baptized here, and Louis XIV took his first communion here. The church has many musical links, too; both Liszt and Berlioz performed in it, and the funeral of Mozart's mother was held here. In a small chapel on the north side, a modern sculpture by the British artist Raymond Mason shows the marketeers packing up their stalls for the last time.

6 **Walk to the back end of the church and take the small exit on the right-hand side, cross rue Montmartre and turn left into rue Montorgueil. Walk past L'Escargot snail restaurant, turn right into rue Étienne Marcel and cross to No. 20, for the Tour 'Jean Sans Peur'.**

This ironically named tower (literally, the tower of fearless John) was built for a man who lived in fear of his life. Having murdered his cousin, the mad king's brother, he dreaded royal retribution. In 1408 he built the tower so that he could sleep safely in a small chamber near the top, while his guards slept below. The tower is now a museum that hosts temporary exhibitions, where you can see medieval latrines and a beautifully carved vault at the top of the spiral staircase.

TOUR 'JEAN SANS PEUR';

WED–SUN 1.30–6; TEL: 01 40 26 20 28; www.tourjeansanspeur.com

7 Return to rue Montorgueil and turn right, following the street. Walk slowly to enjoy this atmospheric market.

Stohrer, on the left, is the oldest pastry shop in Paris, and the 'Rocher de Cancale' is an ancient restaurant, the one-time headquarters of Grimaud de la Reynière (1758-1838), gourmand, author and France's first restaurant critic.

8 Turn left along rue Réaumur and then turn right at rue Vivienne, stopping in front of the Bourse des Valeurs.

The Bourse opened in 1808 during the time of Napoleon and was known as 'The Temple to Money'. The four female figures guarding the two entrances symbolize Commerce, Justice, Industry and Agriculture. Before the days of computers, traders would send messengers careering about with their orders to buy and sell stocks.

9 Walk up rue Vivienne, turning right into rue Feydeau then immediately left into rue des Panoramas. Cross rue St-Marc and enter the passage des Panoramas.

The entrance looks rather unkempt and abandoned but it leads you into a wonderfully old-fashioned labyrinth of 19th-century arcades. The Panoramas were originally theatres where trompe-l'oeil scenes could be viewed as if in 3D, but moving pictures quickly superseded them. On the left you will see Stern, one of the oldest boutiques in Paris, with its original interior. This is a paradise for collectors of old documents, stamps, photos, maps and postcards. In the 1820s and 30s, shopping in covered arcades with lots of small specialist shops was the height of fashion, but the advent of the big department stores led to their demise in the mid-19th century.

10 Leave the arcade and cross boulevard Montmartre, enter Passage Jouffroy and continue through Passage Verdeau. Turn right into rue du Faubourg Montmartre, which takes you to the Grands Boulevards Métro station.

Both these shopping arcades date back to the 1820s. At the entrance to Jouffroy is the Musée Grévin (waxworks museum) which has effigies of famous people, a hall of magic mirrors, historic attractions from the world trade fairs and re-creations of scenes from France's history, such as the story of revolutionary Jean-Paul Marat, who was stabbed in his bathtub. The museum owns the original bath.

Alchemists and Artists

Ancient and modern sit side-by-side in this district. Follow a trail of historic curios, from Paris's oldest house to its Museum of Modern Art.

The name Beaubourg means 'beautiful district', but it was used in derision to describe the noise, filth and congestion of the city's busiest crossroads. Victor Hugo in *Les Misérables* wrote about the squalor of the old streets here. Clearance and rebuilding in the 19th century miraculously left a little maze of medieval streets and monuments, including the oldest house in Paris and the enigmatic Tour St-Jacques. The Centre Pompidou is an architectural marvel and you may like to prolong the walk by going inside to see the art collections. The walk ends at a lesser-known museum that is guaranteed to fascinate the technically minded (Musée des Arts et Métiers). The walk is best done during the day; the area around the place des Innocents is well known for its lunchtime cafés and restaurants. This district is lively, dynamic and essentially young. It is a fashion shopping paradise for teenagers (Punk, Hip Hop, Surf and 'Rude Boy' styles).

Start at Châtelet Métro station in the centre of the square.

Look across the river for a spectacular view of the Conciergerie (see Walk 1). Châtelet means castle, and refers to the fortress that stood here from the 1130s. It became a prison but was demolished in 1806 to create the present-day square. The central column commemorates Napoleonic victories. The figure on top holds laurel wreathes that symbolize fame and glory. On the eastern side is the Théâtre de la Ville, which was owned by the celebrated actress Sarah Bernhardt in the 1890s. She was still acting at the age of 76, despite having her leg amputated. At night she slept in a coffin to help her get used to the idea of dying.

2 Walk up boulevard de Sébastopol and turn right into rue de Rivoli. Walk into square de la Tour St-Jacques.

The Gothic tower is all that remains of a church frequented by the powerful guild of butchers and known as St-Jacques de la Boucherie. The alchemist Nicolas Flamel (c.1330-1418) was buried here, though his tombstone is now in the Cluny Museum. Mystics and mediums meet here; it is also a departure point for the pilgrimage to St-Jacques de Compostella. A fire caused the bells to fall through the tower floors, so it is now hollow inside. Revolutionaries benefited from this by dropping pellets of molten lead from the top of the tower into a vat of water below, in order to make bullets. The scientist Pascal carried out

WHERE TO EAT

🍴 LE HANGAR,
12 Impasse Bertaud;
Tel: 01 42 74 55 44.
Imaginative French cuisine, friendly service.

🍴 THE GEORGE,
6th floor of the Centre Pompidou;
Tel: 01 44 78 47 99.
Fashionable and trendy.

🍴 AUBERGE FLAMEL,
51 rue de Montmorency;
Tel: 01 42 71 77 78.
Dine in the oldest house in Paris.

barometric experiments here in 1648. He also invented the first calculator in history and this can be seen at the museum where the walk ends.

3 Cross the rue de Rivoli and walk up rue Nicolas Flamel, turn right into rue Pernelle (which is named after Flamel's wife). Turn left into rue St-Bon. Climb the steps to rue de la Verrerie, turn left and then right into rue St-Martin. Stop in front of the church of St-Merri on the right.

The church, on one of the oldest streets in Paris, is named after a 7th-century hermit called Mederic. The bell, cast in 1331, is the oldest in Paris. The portal is decorated with curious animals: look for a frog, a lizard and a snail. At the summit of the vault is the mysterious figure of a

DISTANCE 1.8 miles (3km)

ALLOW 2.5 hours

START Chatelet Métro station

FINISH Arts et Métiers Métro station

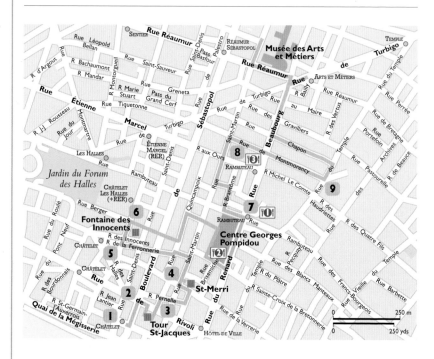

OPPOSITE: THE DEFENDER OF TIME

devil, known as Baphomet. The Knights Templar are said to have worshipped him. Beside the church, from the walls of rue Cloitre St-Merri, fanciful gargoyles stare down. Prostitutes used to frequent the church and a chapel is dedicated to their patron saint, Mary the Egyptian. In his novel *Les Misérables*, Hugo uses the church as the setting for the tragic death of the teenage hero Gavroche.

4 Leave the church and carry on along rue St-Martin to the place

E Michelet. Take rue La Reynie on the left, cross boulevard de Sébastopol and carry straight on along rue de la Ferronnerie, stopping at the coat of arms that is embossed in the pavement.

Crossing the boulevard gives a perspective across the Right Bank to the façade of the Gare de l'Est. This boulevard was created in the mid-19th century to allow north–south passage across the city. It was originally called the Grande Transversale, but was renamed Sébastopol

after the 1854 Anglo-French victory which brought an end to the Crimean war. The coat of arms in the pavement marks the spot where France's popular king, Henry IV, was murdered in 1610. He was returning to the Louvre when his carriage got stuck in a traffic jam due to an accident. He stepped down from his vehicle and was stabbed by a monk called Ravaillac. The king died shortly after and the monk was quartered alive in front of Hôtel de Ville. By macabre coincidence, the café near to where the stabbing took place was called the Café du Coeur Corroné (Crowned Heart); the sign has been re-created, and shows a heart pierced by an arrow, beneath a crown.

5 Walk through the arcade on the right to the place des Innocents.

The square was once an enclosure that contained Paris's principal graveyard. The arcades on the south side of the square (now shops) are the remains of the charnel houses where bones were stacked in their thousands. They were built in the 1160s to separate the communal grave, where bodies were left to decompose, from the fresh produce market at Les Halles. In 1786 the cemetery was closed and the bones of some six million Parisians were transferred to the old quarries, now known as Les Catacombes (see Walk 23). The fountain in the centre, a gift to the city from the king, was used by the prostitutes of the quarter for washing and bathing.

6 Leave the square by its north-east corner, taking rue Berger. A detour into rue St-Denis will give you endless snack and fashion shopping opportunities. Return to rue Berger, cross boulevard Sébastopol and walk along rue Aubry le Boucher. Turn left into rue Quincampoix and right along rue de Venise to the Centre Pompidou.

The controversial Centre Pompidou opened to the public in 1977. A competition was held to design it, which caused great excitement among architects, and 681 plans were entered. The judges liked this one from the beginning. The architects, Richard Rogers and Renzo Piano, designed a building that used the principle of Notre-Dame and its flying buttresses. All the structural elements are on the exterior of the building so that maximum space is freed inside for the galleries. The building is colour coded according to an architect's plan. The moving parts (lifts and escalators) are red, electrical circuits are yellow, green represents water pipes and blue is for air-conditioning ducts. The building houses the Musée National d'Art Moderne, with one of the largest collections of modern art in the world.

CENTRE POMPIDOU;

WED–MON 11–9; TEL: 01 44 78 12 33; www.centrepompidou.fr

7 Walk around the building to the rue Rambuteau, at the north end, and take the small passage Brantôme on the right. At the rue Rambuteau entrance is Zadkine's cubist sculpture, *Prometheus Stealing Fire From Heaven*. Stop at the corner of rue Brantôme and rue Bernard de Clairvaux, to the left.

On the wall is the ingenious mechanical clock that has given its name to this labyrinth of passageways 'The Quartier de l'Horloge'. This strange sculpture comes to life every hour on the hour, when the armed knight, who is known as 'the defender of time', goes into battle with creatures that symbolize three of the elements: a dragon for the earth, a bird for the air and a crab for water. At midday, 6pm and 10pm he fights all three creatures together.

8 Continue along rue Bernard de Clairvaux until rue St-Martin. Turn right, continue to rue de Montmorency, then walk along to No. 51.

The auberge here belonged to Nicolas Flamel, known to millions as a hero in *Harry Potter and the Philosopher's Stone*. Flamel, born in 1330, was a highly educated man. He worked as a scribe and bought and sold ancient manuscripts. He became very wealthy and it was generally believed that he was a successful alchemist who had discovered the Philosopher's Stone. The stone was said to enable the transformation of base metals into gold and give immortality to its keeper, although experiments to find it led to many premature deaths. Whether or not he was an alchemist, Flamel was a generous man and he built the building you see as an almshouse to provide shelter for the poor. It is the oldest house in Paris, dating from around 1400.

9 Continue to rue du Temple, turn left, then first left into rue Chapon. Turn right into rue Beaubourg. You can end the walk at Arts et Métiers Métro station or visit the museum here.

This fascinating museum is dedicated to science, engineering and the technical world. Exhibits include Foucault's pendulum and Marie Antoinette's dulcimer-playing puppet.

Knights and Mansions

The Northern Marais is famous for lovely churches and beautiful homes, but there are traces of its medieval history to be found on this walk.

The Marais was once below the flood plain of the Seine, and the name means the marshes. The first settlers here were groups of Christians who built shrines, abbeys and convents and grew their own fruit and vegetables. The residential quarter developed in the 14th century when the area was protected by a huge city wall, and the lands had been drained. The city wall built in the 1380s ended at the Bastille fortress; the Marais is the quarter between this and the previous 12th-century wall. From the Renaissance onwards a new type of aristocratic residence became fashionable. Wealthy families bought land here and each plot was walled, with an entrance large enough for a horse and carriage to enter. Behind the entrance was a courtyard with carriage-turning space, then stood the house and behind this the garden. The new fashion was to live sandwiched between the space created by courtyard and garden, away from the filth, noise and bustle of Paris streets. These new houses were referred to as hôtels particuliers (private town houses). Many have survived and are now open as museums. There are two fascinating circuits to walk in this district: Walks 5 and 6, which you can link together by starting at St-Paul Métro station.

I Leave St-Paul Métro station and walk along rue St-Antoine, turning left into rue de Sévigné. Take the first right into rue d'Ormesson, stopping in the lovely place du Marché Ste Catherine.

Although there is no longer a market here, the square is surrounded by a plethora of charming restaurants and cafés, including the unusual Double Fond, meaning False Bottom, a café that is run by magicians, who will perform for you.

2 Cross the square and leave by rue Caron, turning right into rue de Jarente then left into rue de Turenne. Turn right into rue des Francs-Bourgeois and continue to place des Vosges.

Walk around the four sides of the square beneath the regal arcades, then stroll into the central garden for the best views of the splendid town houses that surround it. The square was built in 1600–1608, as a country retreat for Henry IV and his courtiers. There are nine houses on each side of the square, the two tallest being the King's Pavilion to the south and the Queen's Pavilion over on the north side. Mme de Sevigné (1626-1696), Cardinal Richelieu, Prime Minister of France, and later Victor Hugo lived here. The house at No. 6 is now the Victor Hugo museum and it can be visited free of charge. There is an ungainly statue of Louis XIII in the centre of the square.

3 Leave the square as you entered, walking along rue des Francs Bourgeois until rue de Sévigné. Turn

WHERE TO EAT

🍽 LE DÔME DU MARAIS,
53 bis rue des Francs-Bourgeois;
Tel: 01 42 74 54 17.
Unique décor from the 1920s.

🍽 MA BOURGOGNE,
19 place des Vosges;
Tel: 01 42 78 44 64.
French cuisine served outdoors.

🍽 L'AS DU FALLAFEL,
34 rue des Rosiers;
Tel: 01 48 87 63 60.
Jewish specialities to eat in or take away.

right and immediately to the left you will see the Musée Carnavalet.

This splendid Renaissance town house was once the home of the witty letter-writer Mme de Sévigné, who recorded in a colourful manner the scandal, gossip and current events of her day. In the courtyard is a splendid bronze statue of Louis XIV, whose court she attended. There is a good bookshop here specializing in the history of Paris. The vast museum has complete interiors salvaged from historic houses torn down during the urban re-development of the mid-19th century. The collections range from displays on prehistoric Paris to the second Empire of Napoleon III.

MUSÉE CARNAVALET;
TUE–SUN 10–6 FREE; TEL: 01 44 59 58 58;
www.paris.org/musees/carnavalet

DISTANCE 1.8 miles (3km)

ALLOW 2.5 hours

START St-Paul Métro station

FINISH Temple Métro station

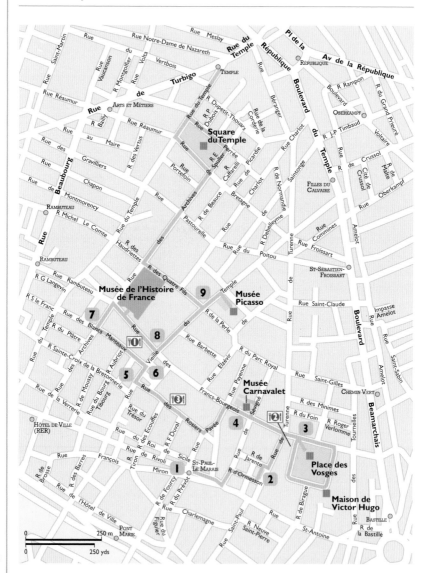

4 Return to rue des Francs Bourgeois and turn right beside the museum, looking into the beautiful courtyard gardens. Take rue Pavée (the first left), then rue des Rosiers, the first right.

This lovely ancient street was originally just inside the city wall of 1180. As no buildings could be built against the wall, the inner space was planted with rose gardens, hence its pretty name. This road is the main street of Paris's Jewish quarter, the Pletzel, meaning plaza or little square. There are several synagogues in the area, and this street is lined with kosher restaurants with delicious eat-in or take-away specialities, including vegetarian falafel and unleavened bread. Most are closed on Saturdays.

5 Continue along rue des Rosiers, stopping at the corner of rue Vieille du Temple. Here, pause to admire No. 47, Hôtel Amelot de Bisseuil.

Beaumarchais (1732-1799) wrote *Le Mariage de Figaro* while living in this Marais mansion. Short of money, but not clever ideas, he set up a business that he used as a cover for selling arms to America during the War of Independence. His natural talents as a spy must have helped him plot the wily moves of his hero Figaro. The splendid doors are carved with gorgons' heads.

6 Turn right into rue Vieille du Temple and then turn left into rue des Blancs Manteaux. Stop at the imposing Mont de Pieté.

Effectively a state-owned-and-managed pawnbrokers, the institution run from this building was an idea of Louis XVI's before the Revolution. The public could bring possessions, have them valued, then borrow money, as collateral. It was hugely successful, and in its first year loaned out 18 million francs in small sums of two to three francs. It still functions today, contracting an average of 500 loans a day. People usually borrow for a month or two, but the record loan is against an umbrella that they kept for 48 years. Mattresses could be pawned, and there is still a mattress-sterilizing machine in the museum here.

7 Continue along the road and turn right into rue des Archives, then go first right into Francs-Bourgeois again, stopping in the courtyard of Les Archives Nationales at No. 60.

39

This palatial mansion is the most splendid in the Marais. It was built for a noble family whose resources had run dry. The lady of the house, Princess de Soubise, wanted to do the best for her family, so she encouraged her husband to stay at his country estate while she had an affair with Louis XIV. She had 11 children, and everyone commented on how number five resembled the king! The pretty red-headed princess later lost a tooth and the king lost interest in her, but before this happened she managed to provide this stunning home for her family, built with the king's money. The building is now the home of the historical archives of France, and open as a museum. Just opposite the main entrance, in a courtyard belonging to the Mont de Pieté, the top of a tower surviving from the 14th-century city wall can be glimpsed.

LES ARCHIVES NATIONALES;
WED–MON 2–5.30; TEL: 01 40 27 60 96

8 Continue along the same road, taking the first left into rue Vieille du Temple. Cross rue de la Perle and go straight on. The mansion garden on your right is that of the Hôtel Salé, today the Musée Picasso.

Built for a tax collector who administered the salt tax for Louis XIV, this grand mansion was the largest house in the Marais until the Soubise Palace (above) was built. The king, jealous of the ostentatious show of wealth displayed by his bankers, publicly disgraced them and confiscated their fortunes. This was the fate of Aubert de Fontenay, who lived

here for a short while, but died in poverty nearby. The building was purchased by the city of Paris shortly after the death of Picasso. The state had inherited a huge collection of Picasso's works in lieu of death duties and the decision was taken to create a museum. It is currently closed for renovation until 2012.

MUSÉE PICASSO;
WED–MON 9.30–6; TEL: 01 42 71 25 21

9 Return to rue de la Perle and turn right into rue des Quatre Fils. Continue, turning right into rue des Archives and along to square du Temple.

Today, all that remains of the medieval castle of the holy Knights Templar Order is the tranquil square and the covered market surrounded by medieval streets. The castle was destroyed after the Revolution, during which it had been a prison. Marie Antoinette and her son Louis XVII were held there. The Knights Templar were founded in 1118, with the stated mission to protect pilgrims on visits to the Holy Land, but the Order soon grew too wealthy and powerful for the king. In a secret operation, Templars were arrested from about 3,000 different locations, at dawn on Friday the 13th, 1307. In the Commandery of Paris, 138 Templars were arrested, including their Grand Master, Jacques de Molay. He was burnt at the stake, and as he died he pronounced his famous curse for evil to swiftly befall those who had wrongly condemned him. The rest of this story is told where it takes place (see Walk 1). The nearest Métro station is Temple.

Saints and Sinners

The beautiful Southern Marais is full of architectural surprises that reveal the history of some of Paris's most famous, and infamous, characters.

In the 1380s, Charles V built a splendid palace here called St Pol. Once the king settled in it, wealthy aristocrats quickly bought up land nearby and built their own grand mansions. The palace eventually consisted of a jumble of these mansions, bought piecemeal by the king, and exotic gardens were created between the buildings, where he could wander in security. Parisians had invaded the old Palais de la Cité during an uprising in 1358. In case this happened again the new Palace of St Pol was linked to the Bastille by a secret passage, and the River Seine offered a royal escape route by boat. This residential quarter continued to develop and prosper until the reign of the Sun King, Louis XIV. When he moved his court to Versailles in 1683, his courtiers followed and new mansions were built, while the old Marais district was abandoned. Eventually, Parisians realized the importance of the architectural heritage of the Marais, and since the 1960s the city has begun to restore many of the beautiful buildings.

| Start at Hôtel de Ville Métro station in front of Hôtel de Ville, the seat of the city's mayor.

This imposing building is a reminder that this square was once the heart of Paris. The River Seine to the south is wide and deep, making a sheltered port between Île de la Cité and the Right Bank. In medieval times, boats using the 500-mile- (800km-) long Seine for transporting merchandise could dock here and unload goods for trade. This square became the central market of Paris. The Hôtel de Ville was built by the city for its chief merchant, who was also the tax collector. Revolutionaries burnt down the original building in 1871, and the present building is a late 19th-century rebuild, nicknamed the 'wedding cake'. Twenty-two colossal copper statues on the rooftop symbolize the regions of France; the reclining male and female figures on either side of the central clock symbolize the Seine and Marne rivers, whose confluence is at the eastern limit of the city.

2 Cross rue de Rivoli, and walk down rue du Temple beside the BHV department store. Turn first right into rue de la Verrerie, and left into rue des Archives. At No. 22-24 is the entrance to Les Billettes.

This atmospheric cloister is used for exhibitions of arts and crafts. It was built in 1427 and is the only complete one to have survived in Paris. The strange story behind this building is that the land was the property of a moneylender called

Jonathas. He was said to have desecrated a holy wafer by piercing it with a knife. It bled, so he then boiled it, but the water turned red with blood. When this was made public he was condemned to death and burnt alive. The church was built here to commemorate the miracle.

3 Leave the Billettes and walk back down rue des Archives, cross rue de Rivoli again and continue on rue de Lobau. Turn left into place St-Gervais and stop to admire the square and the façade of the church before going inside.

In the middle of the square is an elm tree, beneath which local judges convened in order to dispense justice and sort out quarrels and disputes between members of the congregation after church services. The church is mostly 17th century; its classical façade was the first in Paris.

DISTANCE 1.2 miles (2km)

ALLOW 2 hours

START Hôtel de Ville Métro station

FINISH St-Paul Métro station

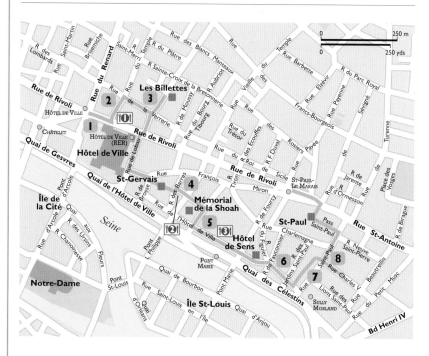

OPPOSITE: ST-GERVAIS & ST-PROTAIS CHURCH

Statues of the two saints to whom the church is dedicated decorate the niches. These saints, St Gervais and St Protais, were twin brothers who converted to Christianity and were martyred for it by the 1st-century Roman Emperor Nero. Inside the church, in the third side chapel on the south side, a modern stained-glass window depicting a sunburst commemorates the lives of some 90 local people who were killed during World War I by missiles fired from 'Big Bertha', the formidable German howitzer (siege gun). At the rear of the church are some wonderful modern stained-glass windows by the artist Sylvie Godin. Godin died aged only 42, shortly after completing this, her last and most spectacular project. In the choir there are some superb stalls sculpted with meaningful scenes from everyday life – look for the medieval butcher roasting meat on a spit, the cobbler with a row of clogs hanging in his shop behind him, the couple bathing together, and the reclining infant leaning on a skull, symbolizing philosophy.

4 Leave the church by its rear exit, left of the main nave. Turn left then first right into rue du Grenier sur l'Eau. Cross rue du Pont Louis Philippe and continue to Le Mémorial de la Shoah (the Jewish Memorial) on the right.

There has been a Jewish community living in Paris since Roman times. In the medieval period, Jews settled in the Marais quarter, which is why the memorial commemorating the atrocities that took place during World War II is here. On the school to the left a plaque attests to the French collaborators' responsibility for the round-ups and assassinations. The long bronze plaque is called the Mur des Justes (Wall of the Righteous). It lists by name the people honoured for helping Jews during the Occupation years.

5 Turn right into rue Geoffroy l'Asnier, then left along rue de l'Hôtel de Ville. Cross rue des Nonnains d'Hyères and continue to square de l'Avé Maria. Look behind you for a magnificent view of Hôtel de Sens.

The Hôtel de Sens is one of the few surviving examples of domestic Gothic architecture in Paris. Built at the end of the 15th century, it was originally the Paris pied-à-terre for the Archbishop of Sens. The building has medieval watchtowers, gargoyles and, at the point of the archway above the main entrance, a triangular opening, originally used for dropping a vertical battering ram. A cannon ball remains lodged in the upper left-hand roof gable.

6 Continue along the rue de l'Avé Maria; the wall in the playground to your left is part of the 12th-century city wall of Paris. Continue a little further, turning left into the Village St-Paul.

This labyrinth of courtyards and passageways was once part of the Hôtel St Pol, built by Charles V. Nothing remains of the original palace but the courtyards are very evocative of the ancient city. Nowadays the area consists of art galleries and antique shops; window shopping is great in this area but there are definitely no bargains to be had.

7 Walk through the main courtyard and continue into a smaller court. Go up the stairs to your right and through the half-timbered passage into a third court. Take the arcade on your right onto rue St-Paul. Cross the street here into rue Charles V and walk along to No. 12 on the left.

The infamous Marquise de Brinvilliers lived in this Marais mansion with its elegant carriage entrance. Her lover was a man called Godon de Ste Croix; with his help, she poisoned her wealthy father, her husband, two brothers and her sister, who was a nun. At this time, poisons were known as 'inheritance powders'. When her lover was found dead in 1672, police discovered recipes for poisons at his home and irrefutable evidence of the Marquise's guilt. Eventually, she was discovered hiding in a convent, forcibly brought back to Paris, and put on trial. She was found guilty, beheaded, then her headless body was burnt at the stake. The witty writer Mme de Sévigné followed the case with interest and wrote: 'It is done, Brinvilliers is in the air everywhere, her poor little body has been thrown, after execution, onto a great fire and the ashes are blowing in the wind; we are forced to breathe them and who knows, through her spirits perhaps we will all unwittingly catch the poisoning fever!'

🍴 BRIOCHE DOREE,
66 rue de Rivoli;
Good bakery with eat-in or take-away facilities.

🍴 L'EBOUILLANTÉ,
6 rue des Barres;
Tel: 01 42 74 70 52.
The speciality is crispy pancakes known as 'Bricks'.

🍴 LE TRUMILOU,
84 quai de l'Hôtel de Ville;
Tel: 01 42 77 63 98.
Old-style traditional French bistro.

8 Walk back to rue St-Paul, turning right. At No. 22 is the Red Wheelbarrow English bookstore. Cross to the left and continue, turning left into the passage St-Paul. Walk through the passage into the church of St-Paul.

The passage St-Paul is an ancient street still lined with bollards to protect buildings and pedestrians from the dangers of iron-rimmed carriage wheels. The church was financed by Louis XIII and built for the Jesuits, whom he favoured. The decorative baroque architecture reflects the new mindset of the age. The two huge conch shell stoops on either side of the main exit were given by Victor Hugo for his daughter's wedding here. End your tour here or continue onto Walk 5. St-Paul Métro station is just to the left of the church.

OVERLEAF: HOTEL DE VILLE

Backstreets of the Bastille

Before the Revolution, the Bastille area was a faubourg (a district outside Paris) and there's still a flavour of the past in its narrow streets.

The Bastille was a massive medieval castle built to defend the Paris of Charles V. It took 13 years to build and was completed in 1382, but took only four months to destroy in 1789. During the reign of Louis XIV the Bastille became notorious as a place where the king could send his enemies without them being tried. The king's infamous 'Lettres de Cachet' were enough to earn someone an indeterminate sentence; among the famous here were the Man in the Iron Mask, the Marquis de Sade, Voltaire and the celebrated Latude, who escaped several times. The poor were kept in dungeons in bad conditions where they were left to starve, or drown when the Seine flooded. Louis XI, the 'Spider King', kept prisoners in tightly fitting cages. Prisoners with money or connections could live well, bringing their own staff and holding sumptuous dinner parties. Some had so much freedom that one of the towers was named the Liberty Tower. To best enjoy this walk, avoid Sunday when the courtyards are closed and the garden is crowded. The morning market is on a Thursday.

From quai de la Rapée Métro station cross the road (pont Morland), go down the steps and walk along beside the canal and its Port de Plaisance.

This pleasant marina provides moorings for boats, some of which are semi-permanent and some are just visiting, lucky enough to find a berth at this prime location. The pretty gardens were planted in the 1980s when the area was gentrified and there is now a café called the Grand Bleu, named after the film, where you can take tea or an ice cream while enjoying the lovely view of the many and various boats. The old walls on the other side of the canal are part of the 14th-century city fortifications. Boats leave from here to go up the canal St-Martin on an enjoyable cruise.

2 Walk up the canalside slope to reach the place de la Bastille.

From here you can see the new opera house, Opéra Bastille, with its elegant modern curving glass front. Venezuelan/Canadian architect Carlos Ott designed the building in the 1980s. It provides 2,700 seats, some at quite reasonable prices, and almost all with perfect visibility. The booking hall is on the right-hand side; sometimes guided tours are available. In the middle of the square is a column to the memory of the Revolution of 1830; the Revolution that saw a king put back on the throne. You can see the dates on the base: July 27-29. On the top is a statue of the Spirit of Liberty holding broken chains. This was

an area quick to participate in uprisings due to the large working class population.

3 Cross boulevard Bourdon and boulevard Henri IV and stand in front of the café Français.

Look on the ground for the paving stones that trace the shape of the Bastille prison, which stood here. The Bastille was a defensive fortress built on the eastern side of the city to protect it from invasion. When Paris grew larger the Bastille was no longer on the outside of the city and it became a prison. At the Revolution of 1789 on 14 July it was stormed by a mob wanting gunpowder for the guns they had raided from Les Invalides. They freed seven prisoners, mostly madmen or murderers, who were astonished to be paraded as heroes. Soon afterwards the building was demolished and the stones were sold off as souvenirs. Bastille Day on 14 July is now a national holiday.

DISTANCE 1.5 miles (2.5km) – plus optional promenade plantée
2.8 miles (4.5km)

ALLOW 2.5 hours

START Quai de la Rapée Métro station

FINISH Gare de Lyon Métro station

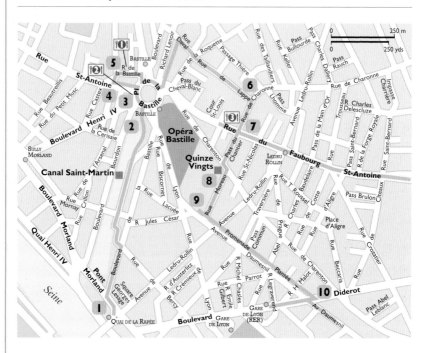

4 Cross rue St-Antoine and turn left. Walk ahead for one block.

A large statue of Pierre-Augustin Caron de Beaumarchais (1732-1799) commemorates the entrepreneur and author of *Le Barbier de Séville* and *Le Mariage de Figaro*, who lived nearby. The works were written as plays but were made into two of the most popular operas of all time; they are often performed at the Bastille.

5 Turn right into rue de la Bastille, walking past Restaurant Bofinger at No. 3. This restaurant has a stunning art nouveau interior and also serves good traditional French brasserie food. Continue walking round the Bastille square. A large fresh produce market is held on boulevard Richard Lenoir on Thursday and Sunday mornings. Turn left into a pretty courtyard, Cour Damoye, and walk along to the end. Turn right into rue de Lappe.

OPPOSITE: FRESH PRODUCE MARKET

Rue de Lappe is very lively in the evenings, with a multitude of restaurants, bars and clubs. Halfway along is an old-style dance hall from the 1930s, the Ballajo, still a popular venue for those who love to dance the tango or rock and roll style. The area used to be famous for its dance halls and an atmosphere in which the rich could enjoy slumming it with the working classes. Shops and restaurants here serve specialities from the Auvergne, an area famous for its galoches (workmen's leather clogs), which are often hung in the windows. Many Parisian restaurants were set up by people from this relatively poor region in the 19th and 20th centuries.

6 At the end of rue de Lappe turn right into rue de Charonne. Cross the rue du Faubourg St-Antoine, and walk along it on the right to No. 46 for the restaurant Barrio Latino.

This unusual restaurant, with its spectacular interior converted from an old furniture showroom, makes an interesting place for lunch. In the evenings it is crowded and a lot more expensive, but at lunchtime it has a reasonably priced menu. Peep in, ask for their card and enjoy the interior décor even if you do not eat here. Turn back and walk into the attractive courtyard at No. 56. There is a second courtyard behind on the right.

7 Turn back down the rue du Faubourg St-Antoine and go into the small passage way on the right.

Passage du Chantier is lined with workshops where small-scale furniture is still made by craftsmen. The area has been associated with the furniture-making business since the 15th century, when Louis XI gave people the right

to set up shop here in a bid to relieve local poverty. At the time, the district was outside Paris. Some of the famous French furniture-makers, such as Weisweiler and Carlin, who produced the masterpieces of the 18th century for Queen Marie Antoinette, had workshops here. Now it is a mixture of brash furniture stores with pieces made cheaply abroad or small artisans making traditional-style pieces. However, the trades of upholstery and gilding have survived in the workshops of the smaller backstreets.

8 Turn left and then turn first right beside a hospital curiously called the Quinze Vingts, meaning 15 x 20.

This name is an old-fashioned way of referring to the '300', a group of blind soldiers housed in a special hospice founded by Louis IX in the 13th century. The institution is now a general hospital specializing in eye disorders. The gateway to the hospital and stone buildings at the entrance were once the quarters of the famous Musketeers in the 18th century. The modern hospital has replaced the other buildings from that era.

9 Walk down rue Moreau, turn right into avenue Daumesnil and then go up the steps to the promenade Plantée.

The attractive raised walkway, planted with greenery and flowers, was built to replace old railway tracks, and a station once stood where the opera house is now. If you wish to go to the end, the walk will take you to the Bois de Vincennes,

WHERE TO EAT

🍽 BOFINGER,
3 rue de la Bastille;
Tel: 01 42 72 87 82.
Art nouveau brasserie.
Reservations recommended.

🍽 CAFÉ FRANÇAIS,
3 place de la Bastille;
For meals, tea, a drink, or delicious snacks and ice creams to take away.

🍽 BARRIO LATINO,
46/48 rue du Faubourg St-Antoine;
Tel: 01 55 78 84 75.
Spectacular interior. Very trendy.

a park just outside the city. The railway tracks were raised because the trains went through a densely populated area. Since the area has been renovated, craftspeople congregate under the walkway.

10 Leave the raised walkway where avenue Daumesnil and boulevard Diderot cross. Walk along avenue Daumesnil and look in the windows under the arcades of the viaduct.

The Viaduc des Arts is a pleasant place to finish your walk. Under the old railway tracks you will find cafés, shops and workshops, where traditional crafts, including pottery, painting, glass blowing, weaving, the restoration of furniture, textiles and musical instruments, are practised and sold. The nearest Métro station is Gare de Lyon.

Home of the Famous Dead

The most sought-after resting place for 19th-century celebrities, this cemetery is a tranquil haven in the heart of the lively metropolis.

Cimetière du Père-Lachaise is more like a Parisian park than a graveyard and it is possible to meander for hours through the alleys and walkways lined with tombs. At Père-Lachaise Métro station a newspaper vendor sells large-scale maps of the cemetery with the most famous names, including Jim Morrison and Edith Piaf, clearly marked. It is worth investing in a detailed map; you can then follow this itinerary and see the famous graves mentioned, but also wander off the set route to discover a few more of the 100,000 Parisians who lie buried here. The cemetery is a marvellous and peaceful museum of monumental sculpture from the early 1800s to the present day. Whether for reasons of ego or sentiment, the monuments eulogize the lives of the dead in tones ranging from poignant through macabre, to humorous. The tombs, visible signs of the grief of those left behind, are powerful reminders of the lives they celebrate.

I From Père-Lachaise Métro station walk straight along boulevard de Ménilmontant to the main entrance to the cemetery on the left-hand side. Stop to admire the doorway, then enter. There are WC facilities just inside to the left. Go straight up the Avenue Principale to the massive Monument aux Morts, stopping for the tomb of Rossini shortly before, on your left.

WALKWAYS LINED WITH TOMBS

This cemetery is not on consecrated ground, which means that people of all races, creeds and colours lie side by side, including suicides. Much of the imagery on the tombs is pagan rather than Christian. Above the main entrance, hourglasses with wings remind the visitor that time is flying by. Wreaths are the symbol of eternity. The amphoras above the doorway represent the jars in which the ancient Greeks kept the ashes of cremated loved ones. The Italian composer Gioacchino Rossini's (1792-1868) tomb is a cenotaph (meaning the grave does not contain the body). The much-loved composer wrote his first opera at 14 and retired at 37, having written his famous works, *Cinderella* and *The Barber of Seville*. He devoted the rest of his life to good living, which probably killed him. The Monument aux Morts was created by Bartholomé, a grieving widowed sculptor. His friend, the painter Degas, suggested he sculpt a memorial for his wife; the result was this work, which was exhibited at the World Trade Fair. The city of Paris purchased it for Père-Lachaise and it now forms the entrance to a chamber containing some 35,000

bodies. The figures represent humanity's march towards death. Men, women and children queue at death's gates, above an angel of afterlife, opening a tomb.

CIMETIÈRE DU PÈRE-LACHAISE;
DAILY 9–5

2 Take the steps up on the right side. The medieval-styled tomb showing a man with hammer and chisel at his feet is that of Bartholomé. At the top of the steps, turn right along avenue de la Chapelle, stopping almost immediately in front of Géricault's tomb.

Etex, a sculptor who also worked on the Arc de Triomphe, sculpted this tomb for the painter Géricault. Shown reclining with palette and brushes, Géricault is best known for the painting, *The Raft of the Medusa*, which is in the Louvre. The painting depicts an actual shipwreck; Géricault interviewed the survivors and

OPPOSITE: CIMETIÈRE DU PÈRE-LACHAISE

DISTANCE 1.2 miles (2km)

ALLOW At least 2 hours

START Pere-Lachaise Métro station

FINISH Pere-Lachaise or Gambetta Métro station

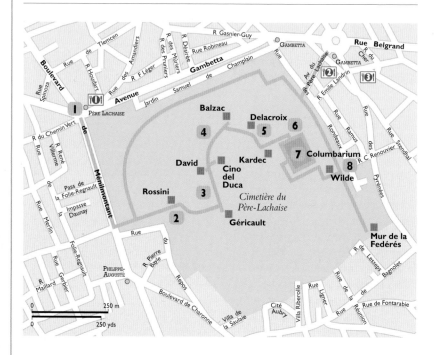

persuaded them to re-enact parts of their story so that he could paint with as much authenticity as possible. He died aged 32 after being thrown from a horse.

3 Turn back along avenue de la Chapelle and walk past the steps now on your left, just past the chapel. On the second set of steps is the tomb containing the heart of David who painted *The Coronation of Napoleon*. Continue until you reach the standing bronze Pietà, tomb of Cino del Duca.

The beautifully sculpted Pietà is unusual in that the Virgin is shown standing rather than sitting. It was made by the Italian sculptor Francesco Messina for Cino del Duca, who died in 1967. A wealthy businessman who owned and bred racehorses, as well as being a publisher, editor and film producer, del Duca's widow established a literary prize in her husband's name. The award is given to authors whose work reflects themes of 'humanism'. In 1985 it was won by the author of *Sophie's Choice*, William Styron.

WHERE TO EAT

🍴 FACTORIE SAINT AMOUR,
2 avenue Gambetta;
Tel: 01 47 97 20 15.
Wine bar serving light lunches.

🍴 AUX RENDEZVOUS DES AMIS,
10 avenue du Père-Lachaise;
Tel: 01 43 58 12 61.
Local traditional eaterie.

🍴 JARDIN DE CHIANG MAI,
28 rue de la cour des Noues;
Tel: 01 47 97 95 95.
Thai food in simple surroundings.

At the time he won the award, Styron was suffering from a mental breakdown and behaved strangely. Once cured, he wrote a moving account of this period of his life called *Darkness Visible*. The book is subtitled 'A Memoir of Madness'.

4 Take the first little alley on the right and continue straight along to the statue of Balzac to the left.

Honoré de Balzac was the author of a great series of novels called collectively *La Comédie humaine* (The Human Comedy). His works consist of some 70 novels about love, intrigue, social climbing and the power of money. Balzac was neither good-looking nor wealthy, but he had a series of love affairs with beautiful women who were mostly married and aristocratic. He corresponded with a Polish countess for

around 20 years. They finally married, and his death followed more or less immediately. The bust of Balzac was sculpted by David d'Angers. Opposite this tomb is the grave of Gérard de Nerval, an eccentric poet and writer, who is known as a precursor of the surrealists. He captured the essence of life in 19th-century Paris in his writings.

5 Turn back then immediately left past the massive tomb of Delacroix. His famous painting *La Liberté guidant le people* (Liberty leading the people) hangs in the Louvre. He also painted the Chapel of the Holy Angels in St Sulpice. Continue, turning right into avenue Transversale No. 1 then first left, stopping to look at the massive tomb of Allan Kardec.

Always covered in floral tributes, this monument is in the form of a dolmen, commemorating the burials of ancient Celtic princes. Allan Kardec founded the doctrine of 'Spiritism' (communicating with the dead). His inscription reads: 'To be born, to die, to be born again and ceaselessly progress – that is the law'. Mediums frequently visit the tomb in order to communicate with their mentor.

6 Continue straight on to the Columbarium on the right.

In the centre of the cemetery is the crematorium. The surrounding pavilions are divided into 50,000 spaces where urns containing ashes can be kept. Go down the steps to the lower level and

take the first corridor to the left. Halfway along you can see the plaque commemorating the opera singer, Maria Callas, although her ashes are no longer kept here. Her urn was stolen and was later discovered hidden in another part of the cemetery. In 1979, her mother hired a plane and scattered her ashes over the Aegean Sea.

7 Isadora Duncan is at the top of the steps above ground level in the south-eastern wing of the Columbarium. Walk behind the crematorium, turn immediately left, then right into Allée Transversale No. 3. Turn left on avenue Carette, for Oscar Wilde on the left.

This massive stone monument commemorating Oscar Wilde is by the sculptor Sir Jacob Epstein (1880–1959) and represents Wilde as a 'flying demon angel'. Originally, the figure had prominent private parts but the sculptor was ordered to cover his work with the addition of a fig leaf. This was later removed by a group of drunken students who returned it to Epstein. The missing bit of the statue is now believed to be a paperweight on the desk of the British Ambassador. Oscar Wilde died in Paris in 1900. At the time he was financially ruined and was originally buried outside Paris in a pauper's grave. Several years later his literary executor, Robert Ross, helped organize the re-burial, choosing Epstein to create the tomb.

8 Continue to the end of the alley. If you turn right here you will pass some interesting tombs and the Mur des Fedérés (Wall of the Federates), where hundreds of Communards were executed after the Siege of Paris in 1871. If you turn left, you can follow the avenue Circulaire back to the main entrance and the Pere-Lachaise Métro station, or the exit to place Gambetta. The Gambetta Métro station is on the right after the 2nd division.

OVERLEAF: FEDERATES WALL AT PERE LACHAISE CEMETERY

61

The Romantic Island

The beautiful Île St-Louis, with its historic town houses, tree-lined quaysides and old bridges, attracts crowds of strollers in spring and summer.

Until the 17th century this island was simply two low-lying mounds that regularly flooded. They were divided by a gully through which ran the Seine. One side was called Île Notre-Dame and belonged to the church, which rented out the land. The other was Île aux Vaches (The Isle of Cows). In the early 17th century, Henry IV ordered the islands to be joined together to create a residential district. This was done rapidly, which accounts for the uniformity of the architecture. The gully was filled, quaysides were built around the island and the Pont Marie bridge was built. The level of the island was raised and divided into a grid pattern of plots. Artisans and shopkeepers flocked to the central street, whereas the nobility chose the riverside plots. The island was densely developed over a period of 50 years then, during the reign of Louis XIV, the elegant residences were gradually abandoned as people moved out to Versailles. By the 19th century Île St-Louis had become one of the poorest quarters in Paris. In the 1920s the area became a favourite with 'the Lost Generation' including Ernest Hemingway, Dos Passos, Nancy Cunard and Helena Rubinstein.

1 Begin the walk from Sully Morland
Métro station.

On your left is a modern statue of the poet Rimbaud (1854-1891) depicted as a flying figure chased by letters of the alphabet. This alludes to a poem he wrote about vowels. Cross to the garden in the centre to see stones from the Bastille fortress, found and moved here when the Métro was built at Bastille square.

2 Cross the bridge ahead of you, Pont Sully, go into the garden on the tip of the island through an entrance on your left.

From this garden, shaded in the summer by large plane trees, there is a splendid view up river. In the distance you can see the modern building of the Finance Ministry, which projects into the river on the Right Bank (on your left as you look up river), and immediately on your right a rather scruffy modern building belonging to the University of Paris. The river bank on the right-hand side has become a modern sculpture park and is a popular place for joggers and walkers.

3 Leave the garden and walk along the south bank of the island, quai de Béthune. Turn first right into rue de Bretonvilliers, through an old archway, before turning right into rue St-Louis en l'Île. Look down the main street for a view of the church with its pierced spire. Continue to the end of the island and turn left into quai d'Anjou. Stop to look at No. 1.

This elegant 17th-century mansion, the Hôtel Lambert, is immense in size and has a long gallery with a decorated bow front. You can just see part of the large garden. The mansion was designed by the men who built the palace of Versailles – architect Le Vau and painter Le Brun, hence its grand style. It was lived in by the writer and philosopher Voltaire (1694-1778), and later by a Polish prince in exile, Prince Czartorisky, whose family were given piano lessons by Chopin. The composer was occasionally persuaded to perform in the great hall. The house now belongs to the Rothschild family.

4 Continue to No. 7, the Bakers' Corporation headquarters (Syndicate des Maitres Boulangers de Paris).

DISTANCE **1.5 miles (2.5km)**

ALLOW **2 hours**

START **Sully Morland Métro station**

FINISH **Pont Marie Métro station**

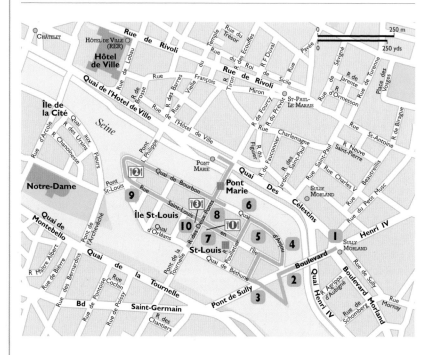

Peep into the entrance hall where you will see old wooden troughs for kneading the dough, and reproductions of plates from the encyclopedia edited by the philosophers of the Enlightenment. Since industrialization, bakers using traditional methods have to fight for survival. Authentic bakers carry the denomination 'artisan boulanger', a badge of quality.

5 At No. 17 you will see the Hôtel de Lauzun with its drainpipes in the shape of fish.

In the 17th century the wealthy owner of this house paid for the elaborate decoration, but when the island went downmarket in the 19th century the premises became a laundry. Having no use for the gilded and painted wood panelling, the owner stored it in the cellars and by good fortune it was salvagable when they came to restore the house. L'Hôtel de Lauzun now belongs to the city of Paris and is used for receptions, at which its ornate decoration is appreciated once more.

6 Turn left into rue Poulletier, which is where the island was once divided into two parts by a moat. Turn right into rue St-Louis en l'Île and enter the church.

This church has suffered from the elements: the original chapel on this spot was struck by lightning, then the spire of the present church was destroyed in a gale, so they re-built it with holes to enable the wind to pass through. The church was dedicated to St Louis. The island, which had previously been called Île Notre-Dame because it once belonged to the canons of Notre-Dame, then took the name of Île St-Louis. Perhaps it was deemed confusing to have an island called Île Notre-Dame when the cathedral of Notre-Dame was situated elsewhere. The church has a fine organ and is known for its high quality concerts.

7 Walk along rue St-Louis en l'Île past the famous ice cream parlour Berthillon. Turn right into rue des Deux Ponts and continue to the middle of the bridge Pont Marie. Enjoy the view of the river and look back at the island.

The road across the island was widened in the 1920s and ugly modern housing built on the left-hand side. Compare this to the charming irregular structures on the right, which date back to the 17th century. The restaurant on the right-hand corner, the Franc Pinot, has an attractive façade with old-style railings and decoration, and an old shop sign depicting a man in a flat-bottomed boat

HOTEL DE LAUZUN

ferrying barrels of wine. At one time, all the shops had these picturesque signs because people couldn't read. This sign is a reminder of the importance of the river for trade and transport. The restaurant holds regular jazz nights.

8 Go back onto the island, turn left for No. 29 quai d'Anjou to see where Hemingway worked editing a literary journal in the 1920s, then go back on your tracks to quai de Bourbon and follow along to the tip of the island.

WHERE TO EAT

🍴 **BERTHILLON,**
31 rue St-Louis en l'Île;
Tel: 01 43 54 31 61.
The ice creams here have become
an institution in Paris.

🍴 **BRASSERIE DE L'ÎLE ST-LOUIS,**
55 quai de Bourbon;
Tel: 01 43 54 02 59.
Old-style and traditional, with
sausages a speciality.

🍴 **L'ILOT VACHE,**
35 rue St-Louis en l'Île;
Tel: 01 46 33 55 16.
Evenings only; fun and friendly.

This pleasant enclave has benches where you can sit under the trees and enjoy the vista upstream. On your right, across the river, is the grandiose Hôtel de Ville, Paris's City Hall.

9 Walk down the main street, rue St-Louis en l'Île, enjoying the variety of small boutiques selling jewellery, fashions, patisserie, ice creams, foie gras, and other specialities. Stop at No. 51, Hôtel Chenizot, and admire its façade from the outside. Inside the courtyard there are fine door handles crafted in the shape of horses.

Built in the 17th century and further embellished in the 18th century, this was once a very fine mansion, the home of a number of wealthy noble families. In the 19th century it became the residence of the Archbishop of Paris, Monseigneur Affre, and it was also the place where Monseigneur Affre was shot dead as he climbed onto a barricade to try to calm the truculent crowd during the Revolution of 1848. Later, the building was much disfigured when it became a gendarmerie. Deep in the centre of the courtyard there is an old sundial in the midst of what was once a beautiful formal garden.

10 Turn right into rue des Deux Ponts, past an old-style restaurant called the Îlot Vache (a pun on the old name of the smaller island, Île aux Vaches). Walk along to the bridge Pont de la Tournelle.

The house on the corner of quai de Béthune and rue des Deux Ponts was lived in by Nobel Prize-winning scientist Marie Curie (1867-1934) for many years. She was the first woman to be ceremonially buried in the Pantheon, along with her husband Pierre Curie, for her services to the advancement of science. On the bridge is a statue of St Genevieve, the patron saint of Paris. Look towards the Left Bank; on the corner of quai de la Tournelle on your left is a top-floor restaurant with panoramic windows affording a superb view of Notre-Dame. This is the famous Tour d'Argent. To end your walk, return straight along rue des Deux Ponts to Pont Marie Métro station.

The Madeleine District

Stroll through an elegant and eclectic mix of architecture and speciality shops, including some of the most famous names in Parisian catering.

Built like a temple, the massive church of La Madeleine dominates the whole district. The building copies the architecture of the ancient world. Emperor Napoleon made a political decision to deliberately use a style that differentiated him from the previous generation of rulers. A well-known French guide book describes the church as standing on a 'parallelipedic peristyle of Hollywoodian steps leading up to the entrance'. The entrance is indeed dramatic and its vast scale certainly humbles the visitor. The view from the entrance across to the National Assembly is spectacular. The Madeleine District is now expensive and chic; the square is lined with upmarket shops and restaurants. Senderens (9 place de la Madeleine), with its beautiful 1900 décor, and the famous art nouveau-style Maxim's are both nearby. There is a museum of art nouveau at Maxim's (www.maxims-artnouveau-musee.com). A colourful flower market enlivens the architecture. The rather melancholic memorial to Louis XVI and Marie Antoinette is open only on Thursday, Friday and Saturday afternoons.

1 Start at St-Augustin Métro station and head towards the large church of St Augustin, passing the statue of St Joan of Arc.

This statue shows one of France's best-loved saints on horseback, dressed in armour, and looking like a tomboy. She led the French armies against the English during the Hundred Years War. The English captured her and burnt her as a witch to discredit her. Some say there was a last-minute substitution and that she managed to survive.

2 Pause to admire the Church of St Augustin.

This is an excellent example of 19th-century architecture. The church looks traditional from the outside but if you step inside you will find that the massive dome is supported by a metallic structure – this would have been considered the height of modernity at the time. The church also had central heating and a powerful organ, both modern in their day, and was built to accommodate the inhabitants of the newly built avenues and boulevards of Napoleon III's Paris.

3 Walk back to the Métro station and along boulevard Haussmann, then turn right into rue Pasquier for the Chapelle Expiatoire and the garden, square Louis XVI.

This quiet garden with its children's play area is used by local people and office workers who eat their sandwiches here

WHERE TO EAT

[O] LE WELCOME CAFÉ,
210 rue de Rivoli;
Tel: 01 42 60 68 53.
Good value lunch and teas.

[O] LE PETIT BERGSON,
10 place Henri Bergson;
Tel: 01 45 22 63 25.
Small local bistro.

[O] ANGELINAS,
226 rue de Rivoli;
Tel: 01 42 60 82 00.
Famous chic tearooms.

on weekdays. The building in the centre is a chapel, built in the early 19th century in memory of the royal family and vicitms of the Revolution. When Louis XVI and Marie Antoinette were executed on place de la Concorde in 1793, they were buried at the nearest graveyard, which was attached to the Madeleine church and situated here. Later, when the royal family was restored, the bodies were exhumed and given a more dignified burial, although it is not definite that the authorities really found the right bodies. The king's special guard of Swiss soldiers, slaughtered during an uprising in 1791 because the king never ordered them to open fire, are also buried here. Louis XVI hesitated to give the order because he did not want to kill his own people, but the Swiss soldiers paid the price.

CHAPELLE EXPIATOIRE;
THU–SAT 1–5; TEL: 01 44 32 18 00

DISTANCE 1.2 miles (2km)

ALLOW 2.5 hours

START St-Augustin Métro station

FINISH Tuileries Métro station

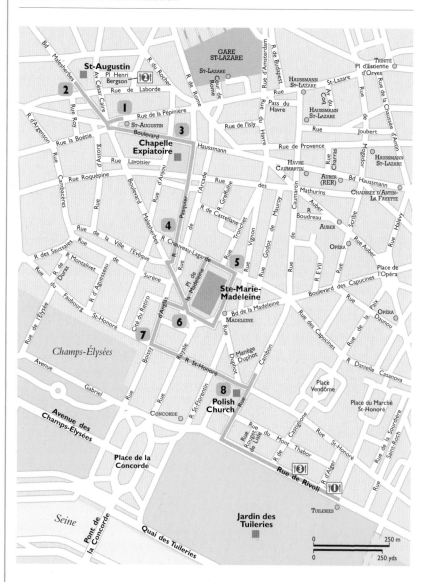

4 Continue along rue Pasquier, turning left at boulevard Malesherbes to reach the church of la Madeleine.

This church is best viewed from the south-east corner of the square, from where you can see both the front and the side. It is designed like a Greek temple, simple in shape and surrounded by massive pillars, and dedicated to St Mary Magdalene. Look at the sculptures in the large pediment on the front. These show Jesus with Mary Magdalene kneeling beside him, entreating him to forgive our sins. The church was originally commissioned by Napoleon as a temple to fame, but he changed his mind and had the structure converted into a church. Inside there is an interesting painting on the ceiling depicting a group of famous saints including St Louis and Joan of Arc. Napoleon himself is there in a mustard-coloured cape at the bottom of the painting. This is a rare painting of the leader, as his image was often removed when he fell from power, or his head replaced by someone else's. The church is famous for its concerts and its powerful organ. Concerts are advertised in the church and tickets are available here. They are usually inexpensive.

ÉGLISE DE LA MADELEINE;
DAILY 9.30–7; TEL: 01 44 51 69 00

5 After exploring the church, take time to admire the environs of place de la Madeleine.

This square is lined with luxury food shops. Maille Mustard from Dijon is at No. 6. Walk round on the right-hand side of the square, enjoy the flower stalls, and admire the mouthwatering displays in the food shop Fauchon, then the chocolatier Mme de Sévigné, whose specialities can be tasted alongside a cup of excellent coffee. On the other side of the square, visit the food halls of Hediard, a truffle shop, a caviar specialist and the Baccarat crystal showrooms. In the afternoon there is often a queue of people waiting at a small kiosk on the square that sells last-minute theatre tickets.

6 Leave place de la Madeleine on the south-west corner and go down the arcade Galerie de la Madeleine. Turn left along rue Boissy d'Anglas and continue until you reach the Hèrmes boutique.

This fashion house is famous for its silk squares with designs based on equestrian harnesses and sadlery. Go inside and browse among fashion items long considered the epitome of conservative French chic. Their large corner window is admired for its elaborate displays.

7 Turn left into rue St-Honoré and walk along.

This road is famous for its upmarket designer shops. If you make a detour to the right you can admire the showrooms of Yves St Laurent, Chloé and Balmain. Continuing left you will see windows displaying the work of some of the younger, up-and-coming designers. Further along rue St-Honoré you will find the Polish church. This fascinating

17th-century church, with its imposing dome, has been adopted by the Polish community living in Paris. There is a statue of Pope John Paul XXIII inside, which is usually decked with beautiful floral tributes.

8 Turn left into rue Cambon to see the famous Chanel boutique. Go back down rue Cambon to the rue de Rivoli. On the corner is WH Smith, the English bookshop, always well stocked with books, newspapers and magazines.

Turn left along rue de Rivoli until you reach No. 226, Angelina's tearoom.

This attractive tearoom is famous for its delicious old-fashioned hot chocolate (à l'ancienne). The thick chocolate paste is served in a silver jug, and you mix it yourself with cream and milk. If you can manage it, try the Mont Blanc gateau made with marron purée. If the queue to be seated is too long, buy a cake to take away and eat it in the Tuileries gardens. Tuileries is the nearest Métro station.

77

Bohemian Montmartre

One of the most charming Parisian districts where you can see the Sacré-Cœur and Moulin Rouge, and stroll through the lanes of the old village.

Montmartre grew on a natural hill made of gypsum rock, which was quarried for centuries to make plaster of Paris. Until the 19th century, it was a rural area with farms and windmills. In the 1860s, the outlying villages were urbanized by the ever-growing capital. As the centre of the city became increasingly bourgeois, the poor were pushed out and began to turn their hands to any trade in order to survive. Montmartre had its fair share of washerwomen, rag pickers, labourers and, of course, prostitutes. Many consoled themselves with alcohol, and cafés and bars, where cheap and strong absinthe could be drunk, proliferated. This new strata of life in Paris fascinated contemporary artists, who came here to paint the local colour. Many well-known impressionist paintings were set here; among the artists who painted this area and its characters were Lautrec, Degas, Renoir and Van Gogh. Later came the modernists, flocking around Picasso, whose first studio in Paris was at the place Emile Goudeau. Spend extra time at the top of the hill from where the view over Paris is astounding. Aim to be at the rue des Abbesses at lunchtime to try one of its many colourful restaurants.

Start at Anvers Métro station. Climb rue de Steinkerque, past the shops selling souvenirs and fabrics. At the top, either take the cable car railway (funiculaire) or walk up the steps to Sacré-Cœur, where you can admire the view and visit the basilica.

Built by subscription after the French defeat by Prussia in 1870, this massive basilica, designed by architect Paul Abadie and largely inspired by the Romanesque basilica, St Front de Perigeux is made from unusually white stone, said to self-clean in the rain. It is dedicated to all the saints of France, who are depicted on a huge mosaic inside. Two statues of the saint protectors of France also stand guard on horseback outside: St Louis holding the Crown of Thorns and St Joan of Arc. The bell tower houses the largest bell in France, big enough for 36 people to stand underneath. When building the church, massive pylons had to be sunk into the nearby hill to support it. American bombs nearly destroyed the church at the end of World War II.

SACRÉ-CŒUR; 6AM–10.30PM; TEL: 01 53 41 89 00; www.sacre-coeur-montmartre.com

2 Leave the Sacré-Cœur, turn right into rue Azais, and then second right, and you will see the small church of St-Pierre on your right.

The plain façade with its modern bronze doors hides an ancient church that once belonged to the Benedictine order of nuns. Their convent stood at the top of the hill. The church was consecrated in 1147 and is one of the oldest in Paris, started 16 years before Notre-Dame. The walls splay outwards under the weight of the roof, showing how necessary the system of buttresses was. The colourful windows are modern, replaced after bomb damage during World War II. The window and the bronze doors tell the story of St Peter, patron of the church. This is now the local parish church.

79

DISTANCE **1.5 miles (2.5km)**

ALLOW **2.5 hours**

START **Anvers Métro station**

FINISH **Blanche Métro station**

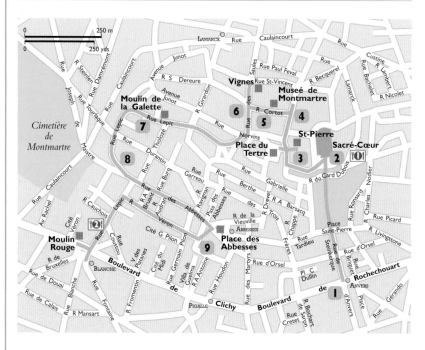

3 From the church go straight ahead to the place du Tertre, famous for its artists and restaurants.

Tertre means summit, and this hilltop area was once the old village square. It buzzes with activity as hundreds of street artists attempt to sell their paintings. The silhouettes made here are named after Frenchman Étienne de Silhouette, who invented the technique in the 18th century. Among the picturesque restaurants on the square is La Mere Catherine, where the word bistro was coined. After the Napoleonic Wars, Russian soldiers came here and called for service, crying 'bistrot', meaning 'quick' in Russian. At the Tourist Office you can buy Montmartre wine. At 50 Euros a bottle it is not cheap but very unusual.

4 Exit the square at the point you came in, turn left and walk past the water tower of Montmartre. Go to the steps and enjoy the view northwards to the town of St-Denis.

In the distance you can see the long green roof and single tower of the basilica of St-Denis, where the kings of France are buried. This was the first Gothic church in France. To the right is the Stade de France, a modern stadium that can accommodate 80,000 and is used for football, athletics and rock concerts.

5 Turn back and go right at rue Cortot, past the Musée de Montmartre with its temporary exhibitions and local history. Turn right into rue des Saules and continue until you reach the vineyard on your right, and the Lapin Agile cabaret ahead.

Vines once covered this hill, at a time when people drank local wines that were rough but cheap and plentiful. One of the streets here is named after the patron saint of wine, St Vincent. The vines disappeared when the land became more valuable for construction, but the local community fought to keep them. The wine festival held every year on the second Saturday of October is an excuse for great merriment, even though the wine is rumoured to be undrinkable! Just below the vineyard stands the picturesque little cabaret bar, the Agile Rabbit, with its sign showing a rabbit running away from the cooking pot. The name is a pun, as the artist who painted the sign was called A. Gill. Many impoverished artists, including Picasso, Modigliani and Utrillo, used to enjoy the show here and pay for their seat with their paintings. Unfortunately the owner sold them before the artists became famous. This is the oldest surviving cabaret in Paris and, although small scale, it is very French and still open to this day.

MUSÉE DE MONTMARTRE;
TUE–SUN 11–6 TEL: 01 49 25 89 37

6 Go up the hill, past the charming little restaurant called 'La Maison

Rose', which is on your right. Turn right at the end, turning back to appreciate the view of the Consulat Restaurant. Turn left down rue Lepic, past the little windmill that advertises a restaurant, until you come to the restaurant called Moulin de la Galette on the right.

The windmill is one of the symbols of Montmartre. The hill of Montmartre was once crowned with mills grinding flour for making bread, as this one did, or gypsum for the famous plaster of Paris. There was a popular dance hall beside this mill in the 19th century and many artists painted the lively scenes. Renoir's large canvas *Le Bal du Moulin de la Galette*, one of the masterpieces of the Musée d'Orsay, was set here.

7 Walk on down rue Lepic to No. 54 where Vincent Van Gogh lived.

Van Gogh's younger brother, Theo, ran an art gallery in Paris and the brothers shared an apartment here for two years (1886–8). Theo died within six months of Vincent and the two brothers are buried together at the village of Auvers. Vincent's paintings of this village can be seen at the Musée d'Orsay.

8 Continue down rue Lepic, which joins rue des Abbesses (a lively neighbourhood shopping street lined with small boutiques and food shops), to the place des Abbesses.

Notice the delightful old Métro exit designed by Hector Guimard, and the

WHERE TO EAT

🔟 L'ÉTÉ EN PENTE DOUCE,
23 rue Muller;
Tel: 01 42 64 02 67.
Housed in an old bakery.

🔟 LE TABAC DES DEUX MOULINS,
15 rue Lepic;
Tel: 01 42 54 90 50.
Drinks and simple meals.

local parish church of St Jean, which both date from 1900 and exemplify the art nouveau style. On the square is an entrance to a garden with a decorative wall bearing the words 'I love you' in 311 languages. It symbolizes romance, street art, and international co-operation.

9 Walk down the steps on the right of the church, turn right into rue Véron and continue to the end. Turn left into rue Lepic. Continue to place Blanche and the Moulin Rouge.

The Moulin Rouge cabaret venue opened in 1889. Its shows were considered outrageous, with scantily clad cancan dancers and an orchestra hidden in a giant elephant. Toulouse-Lautrec made many iconic posters for the shows, especially those starring the dancer La Goulue and her dancing partner, nicknamed the Boneless Man. Edith Piaf performed here in the 1950s and it is still famous for its glitzy shows today. There is a souvenir shop on rue Lepic.

How the Other Half Live

Old-fashioned nannies cosseting children are a familiar sight in this park, but this quiet and very chic residential area is full of surprises.

The Monceau quarter became one of the most sought-after residential districts during Baron Haussmann's redevelopment of Paris in the 19th century. The lovely park, at one time twice its present size, belonged to Philip of Orléans, the cousin of Louis XVI. Both were guillotined during the Revolution. Napoleon III's government kept half of the garden for the creation of a city park, while the remaining plot was sold to a wealthy banker. He divided it up and then sold it off in sections so that the newly rich captains of industry could build beautiful mansions and town houses set in luxuriant private gardens. The name Monceau means little mound and refers to the area that was originally just inside the 18th-century city wall, consisting of a ring of toll barriers. The heavy taxes on goods brought into the city encouraged smuggling, so the gates were heavily policed. Today the area is quiet and expensive; the avenues lined with elegant town houses. Several of the local mansions, owned by wealthy philanthropists, were left to the nation to become some of Paris's most fascinating museums.

1 Start the walk at Monceau Métro
station.

Opposite the Rotunda, which is the entrance to the park, are the spectacular angular apartment façades of Baron Haussmann's period. Haussmann (1809–1891) limited apartment heights to six storeys, with balconies on the second and fifth floors. Where possible, he favoured triangular blocks. The entrance to the park reflects the grandeur and elegance of the quarter. Magnificent ironwork railings have gas lamps incorporated in their design and are embossed with the galleon – the symbol of Paris. The classical rotunda, now the park keeper's lodge and public toilets, was originally a look-out post to enable customs officers to spot smugglers. It was designed by the architect Ledoux, who believed that function fits form. He once designed a brothel in the shape of a huge phallus.

2 Enter the park. On the corner of the first alley to the right is a beautiful Davidia tree. It grows magnificent bracts in spring, which have earned it the name 'handkerchief tree'. Take the second alley to the left, walking past the monument to Maupassant, and continue to the colonnade.

Maupassant wrote about ambition, greed, family quarrels, suicide and sexual deviance. His novels were hugely successful but he squandered money extravagantly until overwork and excessive living led to his death at just 43. The monument represents one

WHERE TO EAT

|◎| L'ÉPICERIE RUSSE,
13 rue de la Terrasse;
Tel: 01 40 54 04 05.
Tasty Russian specialities.

|◎| DEL PAPA,
233bis rue du Faubourg St-Honoré;
Pasta and pizza. Friendly atmosphere.

|◎| LES DOMAINES QUI MONTENT,
22 rue Cardinet;
Tel: 01 42 27 63 96.
Wine bar with home cooking.

of his readers contemplating his work. The lovely colonnaded pond is called the naumachia basin, a name used by the Romans for pools on which they re-created naval battles. The columns are thought to have come from the unfinished mausoleum built by Catherine de Medici for Henry II.

3 Continue along the path, walking beneath the stone portico, the last remaining fragment of the original Hôtel de Ville. Turn left into avenue Velásquez and stop in front of the Musée Cernuschi to the right.

This avenue is lined with magnificent mansions typical of the area. Cernuschi was an Italian banker who took refuge in Paris after the revolution of 1848. This wealthy and erudite politician and economist was passionate about oriental

DISTANCE **1.8 miles (3km)**

ALLOW **2.5 hours**

START **Monceau Métro station**

FINISH **Ternes Métro station**

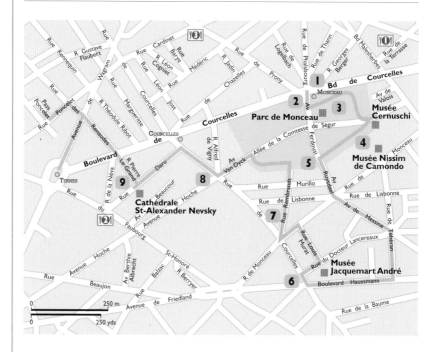

art. He travelled the world, taking an
art advisor with him, amassing a large
collection of Chinese art and specializing
in Neolithic terracottas, bronzes, jade
and ceramics. This mansion was built
to house his collection. The façade pays
tribute to art of the ancient world and
the Renaissance, with its portraits of
Aristotle and Leonardo da Vinci. The
mansion to the left was the home of
Alfred Chauchart. He started life as an
employee in a shop named Poor Devil,
but went on to found one of the city's

most prosperous department stores, the
Grands Magasins du Louvre. He bought
the famous painting *The Angelus* by
Millet, to prevent it from being taken out
of the country. Chauchart's art collection
now hangs in the Musée d'Orsay.
MUSÉE CERNUSCHI; TUE–SUN 10–6;
TEL: 01 53 96 21 50; www.paris.fr

4 Return to the garden, taking allée
Garnerin on the left. Stop behind
the first big house facing the park, the
Musée Nissim de Camondo.

OPPOSITE: CINEMA LA PAGODE

This marvellous museum consists of a private home, built in the style of Louis XV's Petit Trianon in Versailles Gardens, and furnished with a magnificent collection of 18th-century furniture. The Camondo family were immensely wealthy Jewish bankers. Moise de Camondo donated his house and collection to the state in memory of his son, who died in active service during World War I. Later, during World War II, his daughter, son-in-law, and two grandchildren perished at Auschwitz. This fine collection, assembled with great taste and discernment, is presented in 15 elegant rooms spread over two main floors that overlook the gardens. Continue along the alley, named after the world's first parachutist, André-Jacques Garnerin, who landed here after jumping from a hot-air balloon at 1,000ft (304m). Garnerin's wife became the first female parachutist. She went into competition with another woman balloonist, Mme Blanchard, and they fought for glory with ever-more spectacular stunts, but Mme Blanchard went up in a puff of smoke when she set off fireworks from her hot-air balloon.

MUSÉE NISSIM DE CAMONDO;
WED–SUN 10–5; TEL: 01 53 89 06 50; www.ucad.fr

5 Turn left into avenue Ruysdael, cross place Rio de Janeiro and continue along avenue de Messine. Turn right into rue de Teheran and right again along boulevard Haussmann. The Musée Jacquemart André is at No. 158.

This is another splendid museum left to the nation by generous benefactors. Edouard André was an extremely wealthy banker, who had his portrait painted by a female artist, Nélie Jacquemart, in 1872. In 1881 he married her. André and his new wife lived in this sumptuous house, which had been built to house their superb art collection. In 1894, André died and to the horror of his family left his house and fortune to Nélie. She continued to accrue works of art for the next 18 years, in turn leaving them and her fortune to the state when she died. Amongst the masterpieces of the museum are famous works from the Italian Renaissance, and furniture and paintings from 18th-century France. The extraordinary collection even includes three Rembrandts. There is a restaurant that makes an excellent stop for lunch.

MUSÉE JACQUEMART ANDRÉ;

DAILY 10–6; TEL: 01 45 62 11 59;

www.musee-jacquemart-andre.com

6 Turn right into rue du Dr Lancereaux, first left into rue Louis Murat, and left along rue de Monceau. At the end of the street you will see an extraordinary oriental pagoda.

C.T. Loo, the pre-eminent dealer of Chinese antiquities in the first half of the 20th century, started his business in Paris. This pagoda was his shop.

7 Take rue Rembrandt back into the park and take the alley immediately to the left. On your right is the oldest tree here, a plane tree with a circumference of 23ft (7m), which is about 140 years old. Leave the park by allée Comtesse de Ségur on the left. Stop at 5 avenue Van Dyck to view the Menier Mansion.

This luxurious mansion was built for the family of a 19th-century chemist called Augustus Brutus Menier. Looking for a tasty coating for pills and medicine,

Menier blended industrially refined sugar and cocoa solids. This coating was so successful that he began to sell it separately in small bars, thus inventing chocolate as we know it today.

8 Turn right along the rue de Courcelles and left into rue Daru, At No. 12 is the Russian Orthodox Cathedral, St-Alexander Nevsky.

This surprising Russian church, tucked away in a quiet street, was designed by architects from the Academy of Fine Arts in St Petersburg. Its five gilded onion domes symbolize candles; each small spire symbolically burning heavenward represents a flame. Many Russian political exiles lived in Paris before the Revolution, including Trotsky and Lenin. After the Revolution, Tsarist 'White Russians' came to Paris, nobles and generals alike turning their hands to anything to make a living, including taxi driving. Picasso married his first wife, Olga Cocklova, here in the church. The interior is ornately decorated with paintings, icons and gold-backed mosaics. Mass is sung in Russian.

9 Take rue Pierre le Grand opposite the church, cross boulevard de Courcelles and continue along rue des Renaudes. Cross avenue de Wagram to rue Poncelet, turn left, then right into passage Poncelet.

Here is a lively, old-fashioned fresh-produce market, lined with cafés and bars. The nearest Métro station is Ternes.

MOULIN ROUGE
ROCK, FUSION, HARD
TECHNO, HOUSE, DANCE Groove Sex Music
L'ESPACE

The Phantom
of the Opera

Wide boulevards built for carriages are now the setting for grand hotels, refined tearooms, department stores and the stunning Opera House.

This district epitomizes the grand new Paris of Napoleon III and Baron Haussmann, built between 1852 and 1871. At this time much of the old centre was torn down and the ancient winding streets replaced with avenues and boulevards, built to improve traffic circulation and to enable the army to control revolutionaries. During this period a new breed of wealthy industrialist settled in this area. An architectural revolution, especially in plate-glass making, enabled the construction of much larger buildings and this era became the heyday of the grand department stores, theatres, opera houses and railway stations. Charles Garnier's magnificent Opéra Palais Garnier was built at the request of Napoleon III and the avenue de l'Opera was built to enable him to get there directly and in style, although, unfortunately, it was only inaugurated after he had been sent into exile. Although still regal, this historic quarter has not remained in a time warp; the department stores sell the latest fashions, the cafés serve up-to-date cuisine and Opéra Palais Garnier stages some modern productions.

Start at Ste-Trinité Métro station and walk to Trinité church.

This large 19th-century church with its pleasant gardens in front was built at the same period as the Opera House. It has recently been restored to its original splendour with coloured marble and interior gilding.

2 Leave Trinité Church and walk down rue de Mogador to reach boulevard Haussmann.

Two of the most famous Paris department stores, Galleries Lafayette and Printemps, are situated here. The majestic architecture of these buildings, with stained-glass cupolas and graceful metalwork balconies overlooking open-plan shopping areas was inspired by the Paris Opera House and considered the height of modernity in its day. Both stores have tearooms you may like to try.

3 Ahead of you is the famous Opéra Palais Garnier.

The Opera House is one of Paris's most extravagant buildings. Designed by Charles Garnier for the Emperor Napoleon III in the mid-19th century, it dominates this district. The building works were hampered by the discovery of subterranean water. They pumped for 24 hours a day for a year and couldn't get rid of it, so the Opera House stands on an artificial water tank designed by Garnier to stop the water seeping into the foundations. This gave rise to the

WHERE TO EAT

|O| CAFÉ DE LA PAIX,
12 boulevard des Capucines;
Tel: 01 40 07 36 36.
Elegant boulevard café.

|O| BISTROT DES DEUX THEATRES,
18 rue Blanche;
Tel: 01 45 26 41 43.
French food for the theatre crowd.

|O| JEAN PAUL HEVIN,
231 rue St-Honoré;
Tel: 01 55 35 35 96.
Chocolatier and tearoom.

famous story of the disfigured Phantom who haunts the Opera House. On the outside you can see a statue, second from the right on the façade, which shows a group of figures dancing round a leaping winged figure holding a tambourine. The statue was considered scandalous in its day because the women are naked and smiling, enjoying themselves. The Opera House is normally open to the public. If you wish to pay to go inside you will find some splendidly decorated rooms; a magnificent gilt ballroom, which can be hired for fashion shows and receptions; and, if the auditorium is open, you can stand in one of the boxes on the grand circle and see the famous chandelier and the beautiful modern ceiling painted by Marc Chagall in the 1960s. If you don't wish to pay, you can still peep in at the grandiose stairway, with its profusion of coloured marble. Souvenirs can be

OPPOSITE: OPÉRA PALAIS GARNIER

DISTANCE 1.5 miles (2.5km)

ALLOW 2.5 hours

START Ste-Trinité Métro station

FINISH Bowling Green station, 4/5 train

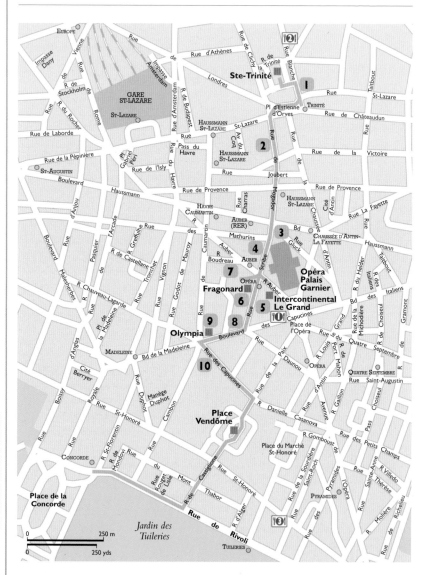

bought at a shop in the entrance lobby, and if you want to try for a ticket, the booking office is on the right.

OPÉRA PALAIS GARNIER;

DAILY 10–4.30 (except special occasions and galas);TEL: 01 41 10 08 10/ 0892 89 90 90; www.opera-de-paris.fr

4 Walk round the Opera House. On the right as you exit is the special entrance designed for the Emperor.

A pavilion projects from the side of the building and two ramps lead up to an entrance decorated with a sculpture of a large eagle. The eagle was the symbol of Empire for Napoleon I and his nephew Napoleon III. The entrance is designed so that carriages could come right into the building, the Emperor could get out protected from the weather, and the carriage could drive out again on the other side. Fifty carriages with courtiers could follow and there would not be a traffic jam. A gilded statue of the architect of the Opera House, Charles Garnier, stands at this entrance. He also designed the Casino at Monte Carlo.

5 The Intercontinental Le Grand Hôtel is opposite this entrance and opposite the hotel entrance at 9 rue Scribe is the Musée Fragonard.

The Intercontinental Le Grand Hôtel was built at the same time as the Opera House, for people travelling in style to Paris on the new railway system, and visiting the World Trade Fair of 1867. If you venture inside you will find a spacious lobby where you can pause for a cup of coffee or tea in elegant surroundings. At the perfume museum you can learn how perfumes are made and admire a collection of exquisite perfume bottles. The museum is free and their shop sells perfumes made at the factory in Grasse in the South of France at very reasonable prices.

6 Go through an alleyway off place Charles Garnier into a quiet pedestrianized backstreet, Impasse Sandrié.

In the evening the two theatres tucked away in this street draw a lively crowd. There are also two large statues here. One is the Greek god Apollo on the winged horse of mythology, Pegasus. Apollo is holding his lyre, fashioned from a turtle's shell. The other one, by sculptor Landowski, is of King Edward VII, son of Queen Victoria. As Prince of Wales he was famous for his love of the city of Paris, where he could escape the stifling atmosphere of his mother's court in England. One of the theatres here is named after him.

7 As you come out of this quiet street, turn right into the boulevard des Capucines, and look across the road slightly to the left at No. 35.

This building has a triangular red gable front in its modern glass façade. This is where the first Impressionist exhibition was held, in the studio of the photographer Nadar (1820-1910). On the front of the building is a little plaque with a representation of Nadar, who was the first person to take a photograph from a hot-air balloon.

8 Turn right here to see the large music hall theatre, Olympia.

At this theatre Edith Piaf performed some of her last concerts with the heartfelt song 'Je ne regrette rien' (I regret nothing). She died tragically young, at 48, prematurely aged by a life of emotional turmoil and drug abuse.

9 Cross the boulevard and go down rue des Capucines. Turn right into rue da La Paix and go into place Vendôme.

This elegant square is the work of the architect Jules Hardouin Mansart (1646-1706), who also designed the church at the Invalides and the hall of mirrors at Versailles. Originally it was built to glorify Louis XIV, the Sun King, and a statue of him on horseback stood in the middle. This statue was melted down during the Revolution and later replaced by the column we see today. The column, inspired by Trajan's column in Rome, has a statue of Napoleon I on the top. It is rather too tall and spoils the original harmony of the square. Look for the sunbursts – symbol of Louis XIV – on the balconies of the houses. On the right is the Ritz Hotel, owned by Mohamed Al Fayed. The hotel has been associated with many famous names including Ernest Hemingway and Coco Chanel, whose shop is just behind on rue Cambon. Princess Diana and Dodie Al Fayed left from the back door of the Ritz for their fatal car journey in 1997.

10 Leave place Vendôme via rue de Castiglione.

Luxury shops are the hallmark of this street. The famous chocolatier Godiva is on the right. Opposite on the left at No. 14 are the attractive displays of perfumes and soaps created by artisan perfumier Annick Goutal. On the corner of rue de Castiglione and rue de Rivoli stands the hotel le Meurice. Charles Dickens stayed here in the 19th century while researching his novel about the years leading up to the French Revolution, *A Tale of Two Cities*. It was also where the German General von Choltitz was quartered when he saved Paris from destruction at the end of World War II. Hitler had given him orders to wire up the city and destroy it, but he was brave enough to disobey. Turn right into rue de Rivoli for Concorde Métro station.

The Golden Triangle

This walk will take you along the western half of Paris's grand processional axis, with a detour into the 'Golden Triangle' of Paris fashion houses.

Napoleon wanted to create a grand open-air theatre where he could choreograph displays to celebrate his military victories. The Champs-Élysées was to be the stage, the Arc de Triomphe the backdrop. In the early 1800s the woodlands to the west of Paris were landscaped into a gentle hill from Concorde to the Étoile. The small, steep streets at the top right-hand end, such as rue de Berry, are where the landfill was dumped. This created a slope, which means that wherever you stand you have a wonderful view. Napoleon's only journey through the Arc de Triomphe and down the Champs-Élysées was made feet first, when he was taken in his coffin to his final resting place at Les Invalides. In the 1980s, President Mitterrand prolonged the historical axis as far as La Défense, the business centre that includes La Grande Arche, although this monument is dedicated to the glories of mankind rather than the military. The Champs-Élysées is still the parade ground for Paris and regular events here are the military parade on 14 July, the Fête de la Musique on 21 June, and the April Marathon. Crowds throng for the finish of the annual Tour de France.

1 Start at Tuileries Métro station. Walk into the middle of the gardens, turn right and walk to place de la Concorde.

Jardin des Tuileries were royal gardens, laid out in front of the Tuileries Palace in the 16th century. Since the 17th century, the public has been able to enjoy them, too. Tuile means a tile, and refers to the kilns that made tiles for the rooftops of Paris that stood here in the Middle Ages. The palace was built for Queen Catherine de Medici in the 16th century, but was burnt to the ground during the Paris Commune in 1871. You will find two art galleries beside the place de la Concorde. The Orangerie, on the river side, holds a fine collection of Impressionist paintings, including Monet's famous work, *Les Nympheas*. It has two large oval rooms creating a complete environment of water lilies. On the rue de Rivoli side, the Jeu de Paume hosts temporary modern art exhibitions. There are several cafés in the gardens, and a great variety of modern sculptures.

2 Climb the ramp to view place de la Concorde from the terrace that overlooks the square.

The land rises here because it is the place where the old city walls once stood. The guillotine occupied this square at the time of the Revolution and over 1,000 people were beheaded in the space of about one year (1793-4), including the king and queen Louis XVI and Marie Antoinette. The guillotine, nicknamed the nation's razor, was named after one

WHERE TO EAT

LA TERRASSE DE POMONE,
🍽 Jardin des Tuileries;
Tel: 01 42 61 22 14.
Brasserie/crêperie with plenty of outdoor seating.

🍽 LE VICTORY,
33 avenue Franklin Roosevelt;
Tel: 01 43 59 47 33.
Local brasserie, lunch or tea stop.

🍽 LADURÉE CHAMPS-ÉLYSÉES,
75 avenue des Champs-Élysées;
Tel: 01 40 75 08 75.
Featured in the film *Marie Antoinette* by Sophia Coppola.

Dr Guillotin, who was horrified that it was given his name. He had promoted it as a humane way of dispatching people, saying that they would feel only a slight tickle on the back of the neck. Luckily for him, he never found out if this was true. In the centre of the square is the obelisk from Luxor, a present to France from Egypt, which at 3,300 years old is Paris's oldest monument. The Arc de Triomphe is visible in the distance.

3 Walk across the square and into the Champs-Élysées Gardens on the right-hand side. Continue until you reach the Palais de l'Élysée on the right.

Champs-Élysées means Fields of Paradise. In the spring and summer these gardens with their beautiful flowers are truly

99

DISTANCE **2.2 miles (3.5km)**

ALLOW **3 hours**

START **Tuileries Métro station**

FINISH **Charles de Gaulle Étoile Métro station**

PRIME MINISTER CLEMENCEAU

Position yourself in the best place to appreciate the dramatic view of the golden dome of Les Invalides.

Les Invalides was built as a military hospital for Louis XIV and is where Napoleon is buried. (See Walk 16.) The ornate bridge is the Pont Alexandre III, and the two large exhibition palaces, with their belle époque decoration, are called the Petit Palais and the Grand Palais. They were built for the World Trade Fair in 1900, as was the bridge. The Petit Palais (on your left) has a large and varied collection of art, from Greek vases to Impressionist paintings, and is free to visit. The Grand Palais (on your right) houses temporary exhibitions. It has a breathtakingly magnificent arching dome of metal and glass that was a marvel of engineering in its day. It is big enough to stand Notre-Dame inside. Two statues are visible from this point. On your right is General de Gaulle, striding purposefully along, and on the left is Prime Minister Clemenceau, wearing a military greatcoat and seeming to emerge from the trenches of World War I.

heavenly. Some splendid gates afford walkers a view of the Élysée Palace, the official residence of the President of France, and its gardens. Outside the gates, in the surrounding public gardens, you will find some small statues commemorating Jean Moulin (1899–1943), leader of the French Resistance during the German Occupation, and a curious statue of President Pompidou emerging from a flowerbed. If you want to look into the courtyard of this grand residence, walk up avenue de Marigny on your right and go round to the front.

4 Stop at the corner of avenue de Marigny and the Champs-Élysées.

5 Walk around the side of the Grand Palais, along avenue du Gen Eisenhower. Turn left into avenue Franklin D Roosevelt to find the entrance to the Palais de la Découverte.

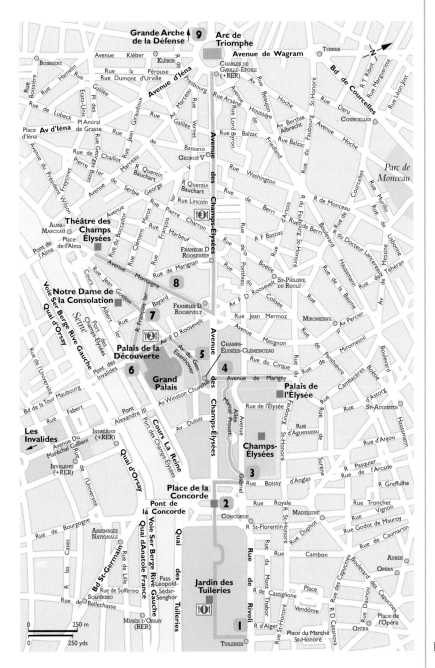

Grande Arche
de la Défense **9**

Arc de
Triomphe

Avenue de Wagram

Parc de
Monceau

Théâtre des
Champs
Élysées **1**

Notre Dame de
la Consolation

Voie Ser Berge Rive Gauche
Quai d'Orsay

Palais de la
Découverte **6**

Grand
Palais

Les
Invalides

Palais de
l'Élysée

Champs-
Élysées

Place de la
Concorde

Pont de
la Concorde

Jardin des
Tuileries

0   250 m

0   250 yds

This museum is dedicated to a lively and interactive approach to science. It has temporary exhibitions and a planetarium.

PALAIS DE LA DÉCOUVERT;
TUE-SUN 10-6; TEL: 01 56 43 20 21;
www.palais-decouverte.fr

6 Cross avenue Franklin D Roosevelt and turn right into rue François Premier. At the pretty square with its fountain, turn left into rue Jean Goujon and stop for the chapel Notre-Dame de la Consolation.

This chapel was built to commemorate 125 people who perished in a fire at the Charity Sale Bazaar, the building that occupied this spot in 1897. A display caught fire, there were no fire escapes, and the aristocratic ladies attending the event were impeded in their attempts at escape by their voluminous fashionable dresses. Many of the women who died came from wealthy families who later financed the building of the chapel in their memory. This terrible event led to the beginning of the identification of bodies using dental records.

7 Go back to place François Premier and turn left into rue François Premier. Stop for avenue Montaigne.

This section of the city is referred to as the 'Golden Triangle' because of the concentration of luxury shops here. If you walk up and down this street you can window shop in many world-renowned stores. Turn left and you will find Dior, Prada, the Plaza Athénée luxury hotel where many celebrities stay, and the Champs–Elysées Theatre, which

LADURÉE CHAMPS-ELYSÉES

specializes in music, opera and dance. The simple design of this art deco structure, with its marble façade and dancing Greek gods, was ahead of its time when it was built in 1911. The Russian ballet dancer Vaslav Nijinsky (1890-1950) shocked the public with his suggestive dancing here, and Josephine Baker (1906-1975), known as the Black Pearl, danced semi-naked, clad only in a wreath of bananas. At the end of the road is the Alma tunnel, where Princess Diana and Dodi Al Fayed were killed in a car crash in 1997. In the opposite direction is Chanel and other designer shops.

8 Follow avenue Montaigne back to the Champs-Elysées, stop at the Rond Point roundabout and admire the plantings, which are changed once a month. Walk up the Champs-Elysées to the Arc de Triomphe. The arch is accessible by an underpass on the right-hand side of the Champs-Elysées.

The Arc de Triomphe was ordered by Napoleon as a monument to the army, but was unfinished in his lifetime. At the time of his wedding to Marie Louise of Austria in 1810, they built a canvas mock-up for him to march through! The statue decorating the right-hand side of the arch (a female figure leading a group of soldiers), by the sculptor François Rude, is called *La Marseillaise,* which is the French national anthem. At the base of the arch is the tomb of the Unknown Soldier. It has a permanently burning flame, rekindled every evening at a ceremony at 6pm. You can climb to the top, from which there is a magnificent view of the avenues leading from the arch, in the shape of a star. This gives the square its original name: Place de l'Étoile.

9 From the Arc de Triomphe you can see in the distance the huge modern arch of la Défense, which is situated just outside Paris, in the business quarter, where it jostles with the skyscrapers. If you take line 1 from Charles de Gaulle Étoile metro station, it takes 15 minutes to get to La Défense. Get off at Grande Arche de la Défense to visit the arch.

This arch, chosen by President Mitterrand, echoes Napoleon's Arc de Triomphe, but celebrates the glory of mankind rather than military victory. It is big enough to stand the Invalides building inside. You can take a lift to the top for a spectacular view over Paris. **GRANDE ARCHE DE LA DÉFENSE;** DAILY 10-7; TEL: 01 49 07 27 27

The Bridges of Paris

Walking against the flow of the Seine towards the historical centre of Paris, this romantic route offers spectacular vistas from the bridges.

The name of the River Seine originates from the Roman word *Sequana*, meaning serpent. The sinuous Seine is a pulsing artery, carrying the lifeblood from which Paris has been nurtured over 2,000 years. Its riverbanks are accessible throughout the year and in the summer and autumn they are filled with sunbathers, picnickers and strollers who seem irresistibly drawn to the edge of the water. In the golden glow of sunset, and again after dark, the river mirrors light emanating from the magnificent riverside monuments, reflecting the change in atmosphere as the workday bustle comes to its end and the city settles to enjoy riverside apéritifs and alfresco dinners. With its mouth at Le Havre in Normandy, the 482-mile (776-km) River Seine is the second longest river in France. Since the origins of Paris to the time of the Renaissance, the river was considered the safest highway across France and was used by royalty, merchants and manufacturers to get from A to B. Today, the river is still used for both commercial and leisure purposes. While you are in Paris, take a cruise on the Seine with Bateaux Mouches, departing from opposite the Eiffel Tower, or by Navettes du Pont Neuf departing from Pont Neuf.

Starting at Invalides Métro station, walk to Pont Alexandre III and cross the bridge.

The Alexander III Bridge, one of the first prefabricated structures in the world, is built from sections of laminated and moulded steel, made at the famous Creusot forge and brought to Paris on barges. It was a technical triumph with its single span taking just 200 days to assemble. The bridge was built to improve access to the Left Bank during the World Trade Fair of 1900. Alexander III laid the first stone in 1896 as part of a pact of alliance between France and Russia after the Franco Prussian wars. The exuberant décor is allegorical and includes ships and river nymphs representing the Seine and the Néva in Russia.

2 Once across the bridge you come to the statue of Churchill. Turn right

along cours la Reine stopping at Pont de la Concorde to admire the spectacular views before crossing back over to the Left Bank.

In front of you the Assemblée Nationale building reflects a mirror image of the Madeleine church on the far side of place de la Concorde. Both these buildings date back to the era of Napoleon I. The National Assembly is the seat of the lower house of French parliament, the upper house being the Senate. Laws are voted here and the building was referred to as the Temple to Law. Until the beginning of the 18th century, the river could only be crossed by boat at this point. The much-needed bridge was built during the Revolution, re-using blocks of cut stone that were rescued from the demolition of the Bastille. The bridge was widened in 1931 and offers breathtaking views both east and west along the river.

DISTANCE **2.2 miles (3.5km)**

ALLOW **2.5 hours (not including interior visit to Musée d'Orsay)**

START **Invalides Métro station**

FINISH **Odéon Métro station**

3 Walk along rue Aristide Briand, which runs alongside the National Assembly. Stop at the little place du Palais Bourbon.

Beautiful mansions from the reign of Louis XVI surround this charming and elegant square. The statue in the centre is an allegory of Law and the square

takes its name from the house that stood on the site now occupied by the Assemblée Nationale. The smaller mansion on the left is called the Hôtel de Lassay and is the residence of the president of the Legislative Assembly. The Assembly consists of the President and 577 deputies, elected from the different political parties.

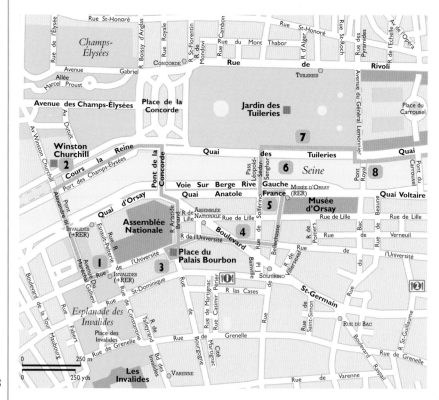

4 Leave the square taking rue de l'Université, then rue de Bellechasse on the left. The beautiful mansion to the left of the Musée d'Orsay is the Musée de la Légion d'Honneur.

The Museum of the Legion of Honour was originally built by a German Prince who went bankrupt, sold the house, then rented it back. In 1795 the property was put up as a prize in a lottery and won by a wigmaker who proclaimed himself a marquis. He was later imprisoned for forgery but escaped, disappearing without further trace.

5 Continue walking to Musée d'Orsay.

This building had a long and chequered history before becoming one of the city's best-loved museums. Plans were drawn up for the site in 1900. The building was initially intended as an exhibition hall for the arts during the 1900 World Trade Fair. The sculptor Rodin was commissioned to make a grand entrance to this Palais des Beaux Arts, for which he created his now famous *Gates of Hell*. The project was abandoned and a railway station, fronted by a luxurious hotel, was built instead. The Orsay station was built and designed for steam trains, but when electric trains replaced them the platforms were not long enough and there was no room to extend the station. The station remained more or less abandoned until the decision was taken in 1977 to create a museum dedicated to the 19th century, thus filling the gap between the collections of the Louvre and the Centre Pompidou. Rather ironically Rodin's *Gates of Hell* eventually found their home in the place for which they were originally intended. Manet's *Olympia*, Renoir's *Moulin de la Galette*, Degas' little dancer sculpture *La Petite Danseuse de 14 Ans*, Whistler's *Portrait of the Painter's Mother* and Van Gogh's *Self-Portrait* are among the many masterpieces on display here. The restaurant, located in the sumptuously decorated dining hall of the old hotel, is delightful. If visiting the museum, don't miss the exuberantly decorated ballroom. The massive sculptures of wild animals at the

WHERE TO EAT

[◯] LE BASILIQUE,
2 rue Casimir Perrier;
Tel: 01 44 18 94 64.
Traditional French cuisine.

[◯] ELLYS ISLAND COFFEE,
5 rue Perronet;
Tel: 01 40 49 08 08.
Snacks and brunch.

main entrance decorated the Trocadero
esplanade during the Trade Fair of 1878.
MUSÉE D'ORSAY; TUE–WED AND FRI–SUN
9.30–6 ,THU 9.30AM–9.45PM;
TEL: 01 40 49 48 14; www.musee-orsay.fr

6 Cross the quai Anatole France and
then cross the Pont de Solferino,
also known as Passerelle Leopold Sedar
Senghor. Cross the footbridge.

Opened in 1999, the bridge spans the
river in a single metal archway measuring
348ft (106m). Its surface is made from
rainforest wood, which caused some
controversy. Thoughtfully placed benches
allow beautiful views along the Seine.

7 The bridge takes you into Jardin
des Tuileries.

Here you can make a detour to visit
the gardens or take refreshments in
the garden tearoom. The gardens are
an open-air sculpture museum where
modern works are exhibited. The
name Tuileries refers to the ancient tile

factories that were once located here.
Tiles for the rooftops of Paris were made
from clay dug from the bed of the Seine.

8 Leave the gardens, crossing the quai
des Tuileries and going down the
steps by Pont Royal to river level. Walk
eastwards passing beneath Pont du
Carrousel and along the quay to the
steps immediately after Pont des Arts.
Climb the steps to cross the bridge.

The bridge spans the River Seine in
nine separate arches; the resulting large
number of arch-supporting piers has
caused numerous boat accidents and the
bridge has suffered serious damage. It was
the first iron bridge in Paris and was built
in 1804 as a pedestrian river crossing. Its
name comes from the Louvre just beside
it, as the Louvre was referred to as the
Palais des Arts when the bridge was built.
The bridge was seriously damaged during
both World War I and II, then in January
1961 a boat damaged the fifth arch, and
in April 1970 a tugboat destroyed the
sixth arch. The chief engineer of Paris
warned the city that the bridge could
not withstand another incident without
considerable restoration, and he was
proved correct when more than half the
bridge collapsed having been hit by a
barge in 1979. The present-day bridge
is the result of re-building eventually
completed in 1984. The views from here
are breathtaking. At the far end is the
French Institute. Walk through the arcade
in the right side of the building and
continue along rue Mazarine to Odéon
Métro station, straight ahead.

Glorifying the Military

Discover the city's military centre around Les Invalides and stroll down elegant avenues named after illustrious war heroes.

Following the many wars of the 17th century, old, wounded or retired soldiers were left to beg for a living or roam the countryside as vagabonds. Louis XIV made a gesture that was unique in this period and built a hospital and barracks for retired soldiers. He chose this area as the site for his monumental military hospital because of its wide open plains, located outside the city limits. The spectacular building was also designed to enhance the king's reputation and glorify his military stature. Hôtel des Invalides was built in three years, opening in 1674. Some 5,000 old and invalid soldiers moved in along with officers, doctors and priests. These pensioners came to be known as 'Grognards' or Grumblers, but they must have liked it well enough because by the end of Louis XIV's reign some 7,000 were living there. Once Les Invalides had been built, other lovely mansions appeared in the now prestigious quarter. Many of the most important French ministries, including the Ministry of Defence, are located here. The Hôtel Matignon, the official residence of the French Prime Minister, is on rue de Varenne where our walk begins.

From Varenne Métro station walk along boulevard des Invalides and turn left into rue de Varenne. Stop outside Musée Rodin at No. 77.

Rodin's sculptures *The Burghers of Calais* and *The Thinker* can be seen from outside the museum. The beautiful Hôtel Biron, now the museum, was built by a man who had made his fortune from wigs. In the 19th century, Rodin rented part of the building as a showroom for his large-scale sculpture. Isadora Duncan had her dance school here and Rodin made many studies of the dancers. When Rodin died, the city inherited his work on condition that a museum was created for it. Many of the pieces are exhibited in the gardens, where there is a pleasant cafeteria. Smaller-scale works and those of Rodin's lover, Camille Claudel, are shown inside the mansion. When their relationship ended, Claudel suffered from a mental breakdown; she destroyed most of her work and spent the last 30 years of her life in an asylum.

MUSÉE RODIN; TUE–SUN 10–5.45; TEL: 01 44 18 61 10; www.musee.rodin.fr

2 Walk back to the boulevard and cross over. Follow the railings of Les Invalides towards the 350-ft (106-m) high gilded dome and go in through the small side gate.

The dome is part of L'Église St Louis, often referred to as L'Église du Dôme. It was built by Jules Hardouin-Mansart, the main architect of Versailles. A museum ticket is needed to visit the interior,

WHERE TO EAT

🔟 GRAND CORONA,
3 place de l'Alma;
Tel: 01 47 20 70 27.
Snacks, meals and a cup of tea.

🔟 LE VAUBAN,
7 place Vauban;
Tel: 01 47 05 52 67.
Traditional brasserie.

🔟 APOLLON,
24 rue Jean Nicot;
Tel: 01 45 55 68 47.
Authentic Greek restaurant, with take-away facilities.

where you can admire the magnificent tomb made for the return of Napoleon's body in 1840. There is a large cavity between the exterior and interior domes, and during the occupation of Paris the French Resistance used this space in which to hide Allied pilots who had crash-landed in France under the noses of the Germans. They could then be smuggled out to 'free France'.

LES INVALIDES; DAILY 10–5; TEL: 0810 11 33 99; www.invalides.org

3 Walk along the path to the left-hand side of the church. This takes you past the cafeteria, the ticket office and the book and gift shop to the 'Cour d'Honneur'.

This magnificent courtyard is reminiscent of monastery cloisters because, before Les

DISTANCE 1.8 miles (3km)

ALLOW 2.5 hours

START Varenne Métro station

FINISH Alma Marceau Métro station

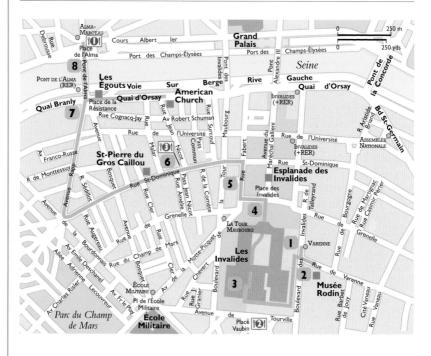

OPPOSITE: LES INVALIDES

Invalides was built, monks were the main providers of medical care. The arcaded courtyard is lined with cannons, many of them captured in battle, the oldest dating back to the 13th century. The four façades are decorated with military trophies representing captured weapons and suits of armour. Beneath the clock on the south side is 'Le Petit Caporal' statue of Napoleon. His men liked to remember him as an inspirational military leader rather than as Emperor. Behind this is the entrance to the Soldier's Church; no

ticket needed. The church is remarkably bright and decorated with flags and other military memorabilia. Behind the altar, notice the baldaquin (ceremonial canopy) above the entrance to Napoleon's tomb, in the adjoining church.

4 Leave the courtyard by the main north-facing portal and walk to the esplanade des Invalides.

The esplanade offers spectacular views across the Seine to the Alexander III

bridge and the Grand and Petit Palais. As you pass through the main arch look back to admire Mars and Athena, the god and goddess of war, guarding each side of the entrance. The dormer windows are sculpted like suits of armour, the topiary shrubs are formed like shells and there is a dry moat outside the main exit. During the 18th century arms were stored here, and on 14 July 1789 revolutionaries took 28,000 rifles then headed towards the Bastille for gunpowder.

5 Turn left across the place des Invalides and right along rue Fabert, then take the second left along rue St-Dominique.

This is a bustling road of local shops specializing in luxury goods, as befits this exclusive quarter. At No. 92 is a church called St-Pierre du Gros Caillou, meaning St Peter of the boulder. This area is referred to as the Gros Caillou because

a massive rock opposite the church at one time marked the limit of the Abbey of St Germain des Prés, owners of the land here until the 17th century. The church dates from the early 19th century. At No. 129 a pretty fountain showing Hygeia, goddess of health, looking after the war-god Mars, dates from 1806. Water was originally pumped to the fountain from a steam machine originally designed to provide water for the nearby École Militaire and Les Invalides.

6 Continue along rue St-Dominique until avenue Rapp, then turn right into the avenue, walking along towards the Seine. Stop at No. 29 to admire the extraordinary art nouveau façade.

This was the home of a ceramicist called Bigot, and was built by the architect Jules Lavirotte (1864-1924). The building is a modern concrete structure decorated with Bigot's ceramics. The motifs are

typical of art nouveau, but also of the style of the architect – sensuous animal and plant forms blend with his subversive sense of the erotic.

7 Walk along to the Seine, turning right along the river bank until you come to the entrance to Les Égouts, the sewers of Paris.

The sewers are open to the public and make a fascinating visit, although it is best to avoid them during really hot spells when the atmosphere can be suffocating. They were built by an engineer called Belgrand during the redevelopment of Paris in the 1850s and 60s. Until this time, raw sewage was put into the Seine, which was also the principal source of drinking water for Parisians. In 1852 some 30,000 Parisians died in a cholera epidemic, pushing the government towards adopting new hygiene measures. The sewer museum is an actual working part of the system staffed by sewage workers. There is an audiovisual display showing how sewers function today, and a small leaflet included with the ticket guides you round. A selection of very unusual gifts is available in the shop! On the south side of the quai d'Orsay is the American Church, located on the corner of rue Jean Nicot. This street is named after the French ambassador who was responsible for bringing tobacco to France in the 1560s. Nicotine was named after him.

LES ÉGOUTS; SAT-WED 11–4 (Closed public holidays and Seine floods); TEL: 01 53 68 27 81; visite-des-egouts@paris.fr

FLAME OF LIBERTY, UNOFFICIAL DIANA MONUMENT

8 Cross the Pont de l'Alma towards the place de l'Alma.

The bridge offers splendid views towards the east and west sides of the city. The Bateaux Mouches cruise boats leave from the Right Bank side of the bridge. The cruise takes about an hour and is a lovely and relaxing way to see Paris, especially by night. The golden flame on the left-hand side is an exact copy of the flame held by the Statue of Liberty in New York and was given as a gift to the city by the *Herald Tribune* newspaper. The original statue was made in France by the sculptor Bartholdi (1834-1904) and later given to the United States. The flame stands above the underpass where Princess Diana was killed and has become an unofficial monument to her memory.

The Iron Lady of Paris

The most Parisian of monuments – the Eiffel Tower – is located amidst open spaces, parks and gardens, making this walk a breath of fresh air.

This area was used for the World Trade Fairs, which took place every 11 years between 1855 and 1937. The last Universal Exposition in Paris was held with the dark clouds of World War II gathering. At this time, two huge and menacing pavilions, that of Russia and that of Germany, stood at Jardins du Trocadéro, either side of the present-day fountains. The glittering trade fairs were organized to show the world that France was at last a politically stable and hard-working industrialized nation. The proof lay in the magnificent displays of art, industry and engineering. And what could better convince the world of France's industrial prowess than the world's tallest tower? In 1889 the Eiffel Tower was unveiled, soaring to 1,000 feet (304m) above Paris. This amazing achievement attracted 32 million people and the city had to modernize its infrastructure in order to cope with the influx of visitors. New roads, the Métro, bridges, railways, hotels, restaurants and even cabarets were the result. The city still has remnants of the World Trade Fairs scattered around in the form of buildings, sculptures and monuments, but none is more spectacular than the Eiffel Tower.

Start the walk from Trocadéro Métro station.

The square offers breathtaking views across the south of Paris, as well as an unforgettable view of the Tower. The name 'Trocadéro' is taken from a fort near Cadiz, successfully captured by the French in 1823. In the centre of the square is an equestrian statue of Marshall Foch, erected on 11 November 1951 for the 33rd anniversary of the Armistice in 1918, and to celebrate the centenary of the marshal's birth. On the wall to the left is a monumental sculpture called *The Glory of the French Army*. It was created by the sculptor Landowski (who made the colossal figure of Christ in Rio) and inaugurated in 1956. The two curving wings of the Palais de Chaillot were designed with a central terrace opening onto a panoramic viewing stage. The palais, built in 1937, is now the location of the Musée de l'Homme (Museum of Mankind) and the Musée de la Marine (Naval Museum).

2 Cross place José Marti, heading to the right, then take rue du Commandant Schlœsing. Go into the Cimetière de Passy.

Take a few moments to wander through this small cemetery. The elegant tombs make fitting resting places for the refined inhabitants of this prestigious quarter. Look for the grave of the pioneer aviator Henry Farman, shown with his hands on a joystick. See the pyramid-shaped tomb of the Comte de Las Cases, who accompanied Napoleon in his exile to St Helena, helping the Emperor to write his memoirs. The painter Manet (1832-1883) and his sister-in-law, the painter Berthe Morisot, are also buried here, as are the composers Fauré and Debussy. A plan of the cemetery showing the main sites is available at the main entrance.

DISTANCE **2.4 miles (4km)**

ALLOW **3 hours**

START **Trocadéro Métro station**

FINISH **École Militaire Métro station**

3 Leave the cemetery, heading for the west wing of Palais de Chaillot, now a museum. Walk around the museum to the gardens and go on downhill towards the Seine and Pont d'Iéna.

These lovely gardens are a labyrinth of meandering pathways and water features. The main fountain basins separate the main garden from the side gardens; when playing, they are mesmerizing, particularly when floodlit at night. The 1937 aquarium, on the east side of the garden, has been renovated and is spectacular, but the entrance fee is high.

4 Cross over onto the Pont d'Iéna, stopping to enjoy fabulous views both east and west.

The bridge is named after a Napoleonic victory in 1806 and looks directly towards École Militaire (the Military Academy), behind the Eiffel Tower, where the Emperor trained as a young man. The bridge crosses the Seine in five 92ft (28m) spans sitting on four piers. The sides are decorated with Napoleonic eagles. During the siege of Paris, the Prussians thought the name Iéna brought back bad memories so they re-named the bridge and removed the eagles. During Louis Philip's reign the bridge's original name and sculptures were reinstated.

5 Continue straight on to reach La Tour Eiffel.

Queues here can be very long. If you wish to go up the Tower, lunchtime or evenings are best. Allow at least an hour and a half for the visit, more on busy days. A small museum on the first floor tells the story of the Tower. You can take lifts or walk up to the first or second level, then take a lift to the top. Tickets are sold separately for each floor. The ride to the top is free if you choose to book lunch at Altitude 95, the restaurant on the first level. Le Jules Verne restaurant is located at the second level, 700 steps up from the first at 377ft (115m); request a window table if booking. Snacks and souvenirs are available at ground level.

LA TOUR EIFFEL; Opening times vary; consult website for seasonal variations.
www.tour-eiffel.fr

6 Walk beneath the Tower, stopping to see the statue of Eiffel by the sculptor Bourdelle, and look up to admire the structure. Walk through the Parc du Champ de Mars to the École Militaire.

On either side of the park are avenue de Suffren and avenue de la Bourdonnais, where some of Paris's most expensive housing can be found. The park is named

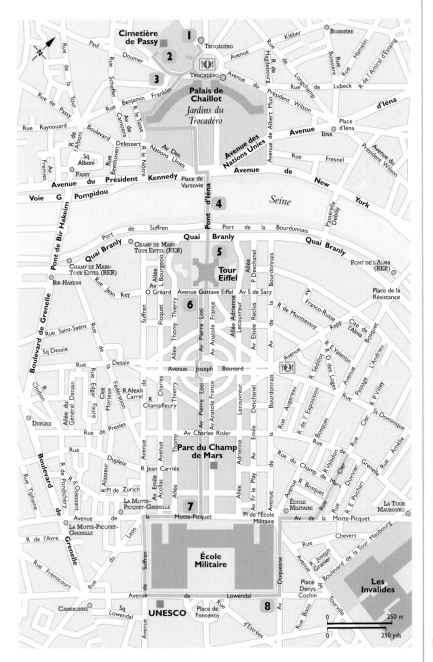

WHERE TO EAT

🍴 **CARETTE,**
4 place du Trocadéro;
Tel: 01 47 27 98 85.
Elegant tearoom; lunches.

🍴 **DOINA,**
149 rue St-Dominique;
Tel: 01 45 50 49 57.
Traditional Romanian, with
generous portions.

after the god of war and was originally a parade ground for the military academy, which is visible at the far end. Up to 10,000 men could practise battle manoeuvres here. The École Militaire has one of the finest 18th-century façades in Paris. The academy was founded to enable young gentlemen from impoverished noble families to become qualified officers. One of the most famous of these gentlemen was the young Napoleon Bonaparte, who came here to study, leaving his island home of Corsica. The young man, about whom a report said 'he could go far under favourable circumstances', proclaimed himself Emperor of the French, aged 34, in 1804.

7 Turn right along the façade of the academy then turn left, walking around the building to place de Fontenoy to view the Cour d'honneur.

This is where, on 5 January 1895, Captain Dreyfus was stripped of his military honours and title. On a freezing snowy morning in front of hundreds of soldiers, the captain was read the court martial's final judgement: 'guilty'. General Darras said for all to hear: 'Dreyfus, you are not fit to wear these arms', then one by one his military insignia was removed: epaulettes, buttons, medals and finally his sword, which the General snapped over his knee. Dreyfus cried out in a voice filled with emotion: 'Soldiers, you are dishonouring an innocent man, vive la France, vive l'armée', but he was drowned out by the crowds who were shouting: 'A Mort! A Mort' (Die! Die!). Dreyfus had been accused of treason. A French document, found in the wastebasket of the military attaché at the German Embassy, was said to have been written by the hand of Dreyfus. The whole of France became emotionally involved in the intrigue and was divided into Dreyfusards and anti-Dreyfusards. False documents had been created to 'prove' his guilt and few Dreyfusards doubted that the case was the result of increasing anti-Semitism at that time. Ten years later, in 1905, Dreyfus was finally officially rehabilitated.

8 Walk along the avenue de Lowendal, the UNESCO building is on the right. Turn left into avenue Duquesne, right into avenue de la Motte-Picquet, and left into rue Cler.

The rue Cler is a wonderful market area. The little streets here are well appointed with cafés, delicatessens, cheese shops, and general fresh produce shops and stalls. Turn right at the south end of rue Cler for École Militaire Métro station.

Art Nouveau to Art Deco

Anyone keen on architecture in general and art nouveau in particular will enjoy this walk through Paris's most prestigious residential quarter.

More than half of the city's government embassies are located here in the chic 16th district. When Louis XIV moved to Versailles in the 1680s, Paris naturally began to spread out towards the new royal town. This district, originally outside the city wall, was known for its open spaces gently sloping down towards the Seine. There were several monasteries here and the monks used the plentiful fresh spring water to make wine from the crops of the local vineyards. The kings used to stop at the Passy Abbey to buy their wines on the way from Paris to Versailles. The area continued to develop as the wealthy bought large plots of land and commissioned the best architects to build them houses. The district was chosen because, being outside the city wall, it was not subject to heavy taxes. At the end of the 19th century Hector Guimard (1867-1942), France's greatest art nouveau architect, built many flamboyant and sometimes outrageous houses here. In the early 1920s the modernists Le Corbusier and Mallet-Stevens chose this area in which to build their extraordinary cubist villas.

1 Start the walk from Ranelagh Métro station, named after an English lord.

The station takes its name from Lord Ranelagh, creator of a refined pleasure garden in Chelsea, London. The Musée Marmottan, located in the nearby garden, has Monet's famous painting *Impression: Sunrise* in its collections. You can make a detour there at the end of the walk, and also take in the park attractions.

2 Walk down rue du Ranelagh, past the luxurious private villas of Hameau de Boulainvilliers. Turn right into rue de Boulainvilliers, stopping at the junction with rue la Fontaine.

The huge circular building on your right, Maison de Radio-France, nicknamed 'The Camembert' because of its shape, is broadcasting house for French radio. Designed by architect Henry Bernard (1912-1994), construction work began in 1956 and took seven years to complete. Now 3,500 members of staff, including two symphony orchestras and a choir, share 1,000 offices, 70 studios and three grand concert halls. The building's architecture is typical of the Cold War period. Like a medieval fortress, the building is circular with a central 22-storey tower. The complex is self-sufficient, having its own 1508-ft (550-m) deep artesian well that provides heating and cooling systems. Beneath the building is the President's Bunker, for use by the President and important members of the government in the event of a nuclear attack on Paris.

WHERE TO EAT

🍽️ RESTAURANT CHAUMETTE,
7 rue Gros;
Tel: 01 42 88 29 27.
Contemporary French, friendly.

🍽️ NERO,
3 place de Passy;
Tel: 01 42 88 15 19.
Good for brunch; lively.

🍽️ CHEZ YANNICK,
33 rue Jean de l'Annonciation;
Tel: 01 46 47 70 34.
Sweet and savoury pancakes.

3 Walk along rue la Fontaine stopping opposite No. 14 Castel Béranger.

This block of 36 apartments is the most extravagant and playful of Hector Guimard's (1867-1942) art nouveau designs and demonstrates the young architect's debt to the Gothic revival. The fanciful ironwork doorway illustrates why the French refer to art nouveau as 'the noodle style'. The façade makes use of different materials; the ground floor is built of costly cut stone, and the upper floors use less expensive brick to underline the difference between the domestic and functional space of the structure. The extraordinary ironwork shows how the source of inspiration for art nouveau is plant and animal forms. Cast-iron sea horses climb up the building like elegant Gothic gargoyles. Look inside the entrance lobby at the

DISTANCE **1.5 miles (2.5km)**

ALLOW **2 hours**

START **Ranelagh Métro station**

FINISH **Ranelagh Métro station**

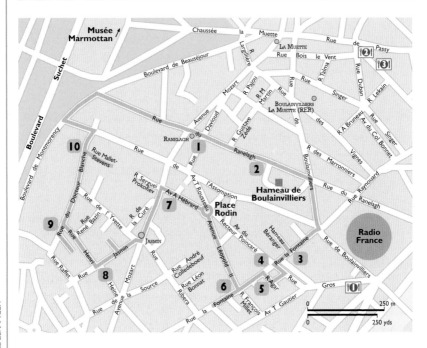

OPPOSITE: SEAHORSE DECORATION ON 14 CASTEL BÉRANGER

stained glass and brass door handles, in characteristic 'whiplash' curves. In the small side street, Hameau Béranger, the servant's entrance can be seen. The balconies here are decorated with a portrait mask of the architect and above the window of the left-hand uppermost apartment there is a huge peacock fan. On the lookout tower of the corner apartment is a mysterious Gothic devil, which caused Parisians to name this award-winning building 'La Maison du Diable' (The Devil's House).

4 Continue along rue la Fontaine, stopping at rue Gros for a superb view of another Guimard apartment complex.

These apartments were built between 1909–1911 and show a more restrained approach. Guimard had been criticized by the modernist thinkers for extravagance and superficiality, and by this period he was battling against new styles in which technique, functionality and modern materials would supersede the ideals of

aesthetic and decorative architecture. The front of the building nevertheless bears Guimard's unmistakable plant-inspired curved forms, and the ironwork is restrained but still art nouveau in style. The architect has not used colour in the same way as at Castel Béranger, but, like the former, the façade is built of expensive cut stone whereas the sides and rear are built of plain brick.

5 Walk down rue Gros, turning right into rue Agar and continue around the building to return to rue la Fontaine. Note the cast-iron drain pipes, house numbers and the road sign, all designed by Guimard. Continue along rue la Fontaine, stopping opposite No. 60, Hôtel Mezzara.

This luxurious private town house was built for wealthy industrialist Paul Mezzara, who made his fortune by inventing a machine that mechanically reproduced lace. Mezzara was a cultivated man who craved modernity. Guimard designed his large mansion with a private rear garden, a ballroom and a separate servants' entrance in a medieval-styled tower. The architect also used glass bricks here for the first time, and incorporated interior doors – innovative in their day – that slide open, disappearing into the thickness of the walls. The house is now student accommodation, but during school holidays, artists inspired by art nouveau style show their works here. The exhibitions are free and offer a unique opportunity to see a beautifully preserved art nouveau interior.

6 Double back along rue la Fontaine, turning left into avenue Léopold II. Stop in the middle of place Rodin.

Here you can see one of Rodin's early works, *The Bronze Age*. This sculpture was inspired by a live model and entered into the official salon competition, but the judges believed Rodin had simply made a cast of his model's body. In indignation, Rodin actually made a cast so that the judges could compare the work of art with the cast, but the judges refused to view it. Ironically, the statue symbolizes the awakening of mankind.

7 Walk up avenue Adrien Hébrard, turn left into avenue Mozart, then right into rue Jasmin. Take the first right into square Jasmin.

Guimard built an experimental house at No. 3 square Jasmin as part of a project to solve the housing crisis caused by World War I. This is effectively a prefabricated house that could easily be assembled by a non-specialist; a 'kit home' that you did not even need a tape measure to help you assemble. The house was designed in 1922 and is much more sober and severe than his colourful and exuberant early buildings. Despite the ease of building and the cost-effectiveness, Guimard's 'prefabs' did not catch on.

8 Continue along rue Jasmin, then turn right into rue Henri Heine.

At No. 18, another Guimard apartment block demonstrates the architect's stylistic

evolution. This building, from 1926, returns to a strict vertical symmetry that moves away from art nouveau towards the newly popular art deco style. Guimard lived here for a while with his wife, Adeline Oppenheim, who was the daughter of a wealthy Jewish banker. The couple left Paris during the Occupation years and Guimard died in New York in 1943, having seen art nouveau derided as ridiculous and old-fashioned.

9 Continue to the end of the road, turn left into rue du Dr Blanche, then turn left into square du Dr Blanche.

The two adjoining villas at the far end of the square were built by the architect Le Corbusier (1887-1965). These cubist houses with their sheer walls, horizontal bands of windows and lack of decoration, far removed from styles previously admired, were viewed as rather shocking. Le Corbusier's motto was 'The house should be a machine to live in'. The end building on raised stilts was built for a collector of modern art; the sweeping row of windows illuminates the art gallery. The buildings are open to the public (closed Sundays and holidays).

10 Leave the square and turn right into rue du Dr Blanche. Take the third right into rue Mallet-Stevens. To return to metro Ranelagh, turn right, then left into rue de l'Assomption, right into boulevard de Montmorency, then turn right along rue du Ranelagh, admiring the magnificent villas. The Ranelagh Métro station is straight ahead.

Rue Mallet-Stevens was built in 1925, the result of a meeting between architect Mallet-Stevens and a wealthy industrialist who wanted to build a residential park for his friends, who were artists, film directors, musicians and sculptors. Mallet-Stevens built in cubes and cylinders of concrete, decorating the buildings with cubist stained-glass windows. The buildings all have a smooth finish and none of the decorative elements associated with previous architecture. The architect's workshop was at No. 12.

Following the Rose Line

This walk leads you through the beautiful Jardin du Luxembourg to two churches steeped in mystery that inspired Dan Brown's *The Da Vinci Code*.
The St-Germain-des-Prés district is one of the many 'villages' that make up the city's celebrated Latin Quarter. This is the heart of intellectual Paris, home of writers, philosophers and artists. Since the Middle Ages, scholars have gathered here in the university quarter; it is because Latin was used as the language of learning that the area gained its name. Districts of Paris have been referred to as 'quarters' since Roman times because the Romans divided their cities into four sections. This area, associated with famous writers, is the centre of the book trade. Literary people browse the stores that line the medieval streets and alleys. Nowadays the area is chic and expensive; St-Germain-des-Prés has shops, markets and an endless choice of restaurants. From spring onwards the cafés spill onto the pavements, and become one of the best places for people-watching. The quarter is full of aspiring writers scribbling in notebooks over a glass of wine. Do the walk in the morning and have lunch in the area.

I Start at Luxembourg RER station, walk around the square to take in the view of the Panthéon along the rue Soufflot. (For information on the Panthéon, see Walk 21.) Cross place Edmond Rostand, continuing around the fountain to the main entrance of the Jardin du Luxembourg on the boulevard St-Michel, then enter the garden.

In medieval times this was a wasteland, a lair for thieves and outlaws, including the infamous and darkly mysterious highwayman known as Vauvert, who terrorized Parisians. Take the allée des Quinconces and turn right to the Fontaine de Médicis (Allée de l'Odéon). This cleverly designed fountain creates a strange optical illusion, making it look as though the surface of the water is sloping. The sculpted figures at the far end are characters from Greek mythology. The Palais du Luxembourg was built for Louis XIII's mother, Marie de Medici, in 1615, but she did not stay here long. In 1630 she was banished from France by her son. Just before the park exit, slightly to the right, is a small copy of the Statue of Liberty. The original was made in Paris by the sculptor Bartholdi with help from engineer Gustave Eiffel.

2 Leave the gardens at the far end of the central alley by which you came in. Turn right along the rue Guynemer and continue to rue de Vaugirard. Opposite, at No. 58, is the apartment where F. Scott Fitzgerald was living while writing *Tender is the Night*. Turn right into rue de Vaugirard; on your left is rue

Férou. The writer Ernest Hemingway lived in the mansion at No. 6 with his second wife, Pauline. Return to rue de Vaugirard and stop opposite the main entrance to the Luxembourg Palace.

The palace entrance is a rare example of Italianate-style architecture in Paris. The impressive ribbed columns were copied from the Pitti Palace in Florence, and built for the Queen to remind her of her childhood home. Although abandoned, the palace remained crown property until the French Revolution. During the Terror (1794) it became a prison. The painter David, journalist Camille Desmoulins and other activists were among those detained here.

3 Turn left down the rue de Tournon and take the first left into rue St-Sulpice. Walk alongside the church of St-Sulpice until you come to the façade. Stop in the square to admire it. Go inside through the right-hand door.

DISTANCE **1.8 miles (3km)**

ALLOW **2.5 hours**

START **Luxembourg RER station**

FINISH **St-Germain-des-Prés Métro station**

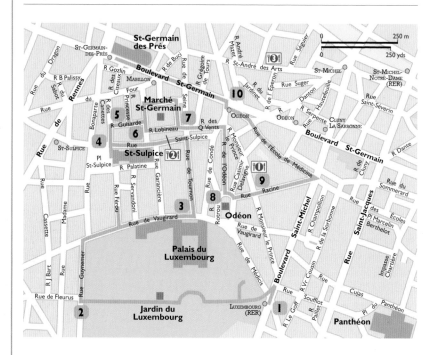

This church is central to *The Da Vinci Code*. It is here that the meridian line crosses Paris, and inside the church is the mysterious gnomon. St-Sulpice is built on a scale comparable to that of Notre-Dame, and reflects the fact that this area became a wealthy aristocratic district in the 17th century. The church porch is massive. Above the central door, a faint and ghostly inscription serves as a reminder that during the Revolution the building became a pagan temple dedicated to 'The supreme being and

the immortality of the soul'. The first side chapel on the right as you enter has fresco paintings by Delacroix. Inside the chapel to the left you will see Jacob wrestling with the Angel, and to the right, the story of a pagan thief called Heliodorus who, having stolen treasure from the temple, is struck down dead by Archangel Gabriel on horseback.

The gnomon at the transept crossing is a large-scale sundial. It consists of a white marble obelisk in the north transept, inlaid with a brass line that crosses the

floor along Paris's original north/south meridian. From this, the obelisk is linked to a square plaque. An optical device in the south transept window originally focused the sun's rays on the gnomon. The lens is now missing but, on the summer solstice, a disc of light falls on the floor plaque, and at the winter solstice it falls upon the obelisk. During the spring and autumn equinox the oval plaque in front of the altar is illuminated.

The massive marble statue of the Virgin, in the Lady Chapel, is by the sculptor Pigalle (1714–1785). Trapdoors lead down to the burial crypt where, from about 1740 to 1790, some 5,000 bodies were buried. The revolutionary St-Just held secret meetings there.

4 Leave the church and turn right into the rue des Canettes.

This charming street takes its name from the sculpted crest on the front of No. 18, which depicts four ducklings swimming on a pond. The road dates from the early 17th century. No. 17 was lived in by the husband of the Comtesse de la Motte, a talented confidence trickster, who swindled a set of priceless diamonds out of a jeweller having convinced him they were for Marie Antoinette.

5 Take the first right into rue Guisarde, lined with restaurants, and then turn left into rue Princesse.

This is another 17th-century street and was home to the famous painter Chardin (1699–1779). At No. 6 is the Village Voice English Language bookshop.

6 Return to rue Guisarde and continue along to Marché St-Germain.

This is one of the oldest covered markets in Paris. It has been completely restored

and today offers clothes and food shops. At the Nicolas wine bar wine can be tasted and purchased. Walk around the arcades of the market. Opposite the west side is the unusual 'Musée du Compagnonage' where masterpieces made by craftsmen training to become members of the craft guilds are exhibited.

7 Having explored the market, return to the rue Lobineau side, continue until rue des Quatre Vents and stop at the Carrefour de l'Odéon (crossroads). Turn right into rue de l'Odéon.

The rue de l'Odéon is a literary Mecca. At No. 9 lived the editor Robert McAlmon, who published Hemingway's first book and Gertrude Stein's *The Making of Americans.* Sylvia Beach had her bookshop 'Shakespeare and Company' at No. 12, and from here she published James Joyce's scandalous book *Ulysses.* Hemingway, T.S. Elliot, Ezra Pound, Joyce, Scott Fitzgerald and John Dos Passos all benefited from her patronage.

8 Continue to place de l'Odéon, which provides an excellent vista of the Théâtre de l'Odéon.

Beaumarchais's popular comedy *Le Mariage de Figaro* opened here in 1784. The theatre was occupied by students during the revolution of May 1968 and was badly damaged.

9 Take rue Racine as far as boulevard St-Michel, then turn immediately left into rue de l'École de Médicine.

WHERE TO EAT

🍴 POLIDOR,
41 rue Monsieur le Prince;
Tel: 01 43 26 95 34.
Lots of atmosphere.

🍴 LE PETIT VATEL,
5 rue Lobineau;
Tel: 01 43 54 28 49.
Small-scale, old-style bistro.

🍴 LA JACOBINE,
59 rue St-André des Arts;
Tel: 01 46 34 15 95.
Salads and teas.

The medical school is at No. 12. The carved triangular pediment above the entrance shows infants stacking piles of books and carrying out an operation, symbolizing the theory and the practice that are taught here. The medical school's museum has exhibits such as the instruments used for Napoleon's autopsy.

10 Continue to the end of the road then join boulevard St-Germain. Cross over and keep walking until you reach St-Germain des Prés Church.

This church is one of the oldest in Paris, a rare example of the Norman architectural style. Merovingian kings were buried here, and are named in Dan Brown's *The Da Vinci Code* as the descendants of Christ. Opposite the church are the famous literary cafés Les Deux Magots and the Brasserie Lipp.

From Romans to the Revolution

Around Paris's 12th-century city wall you can trace the Romans' route, the birth of La Sorbonne and the inventor of the Guillotine.

The old Latin Quarter is a maze of streets that have grown up around the medieval Sorbonne University. It is still the haunt of students and is therefore young, dynamic and extremely lively. You will be walking the streets trodden by thinkers, philosophers, poets, theologians and artists. Dante wrote his *Inferno* while here, and Picasso painted his famous mural *Guernica*. This ancient part of the capital was the centre of Roman Paris and spectacular remains have survived. The Roman capital with a population of about 20,000 was called *Lutetia* (born of the waters), an appropriate name for a city that began on an island. Its centre was the crossroads now formed by rue des Écoles and rue St-Jacques. The Romans didn't build on the Right Bank because it was beneath the flood plain of the Seine. In the 4th century, they dismantled many of their monuments, taking the stone to Île de la Cité to build the city's first wall. Luckily, both the Roman Baths and the Arenas survived.

1 From St-Michel Métro station walk into place St-Michel.

The imposing fountain represents St Michael, leader of the celestial armies, fighting the Devil. St Michael is the patron saint of the French military. The square has been associated with him since the Middle Ages, but the surrounding architecture dates from the 1860s. Marble plaques record the names of soldiers who fell as the Allied tanks rumbled down the boulevard during the Liberation in August 1944. Opened in 1910, the Métro line at place St-Michel was the first to cross the Seine. The station took four years to construct and was built above ground then lowered into position.

2 Leave the square by rue St-André des Arts. Walk to rue des Grands Augustins on the right, turn into the street and continue to No. 7.

This is where Picasso (1881-1973) lived with his young lover, Françoise Gilot, and where he painted *Guernica*.

3 Go back and take the first right, rue Christine, and cross rue Dauphine into the passage Dauphine. On leaving the passage turn right into rue Mazarine, left into Jacques Callot and left again into rue de Seine. Turn immediately right into rue de l'Echaudé, right into rue Jacob and first left into rue Furstemberg.

The attractive place Furstemberg was once the stables of the Abbey of St-Germain-des-Prés. Looking across the

WHERE TO EAT

🍴 CRÊPERIE DE CLUNY,
20 rue de la Harpe;
Tel: 01 43 26 08 38.
The speciality is pancakes.

🍴 LES DEGRÉS DE NOTRE-DAME,
10 rue des Grands Degrés;
Tel: 01 55 42 88 88.
Mixture of traditional French and North African cuisine.

🍴 LA FOURMI AILÉ,
8 rue du Fouarre;
Tel: 01 43 29 40 99.
Tearoom serving lunches.

square you can admire the handsome brick and stone façade of the Abbots' Palace. The Musée Delacroix is located in the corner of the square. Delacroix's (1798-1863) most celebrated painting in the Louvre is *Liberty Leading the People*.

4 Leave the square by the rue Cardinale, then rue de Bourbon le Château. Turn left into rue de Buci, continue until the crossroads, then go straight on into rue St-André des Arts. Take the first right into the covered arcade Cour du Commerce St-André.

Le Procope (to the right) claims to be the oldest coffee house in Paris, and was the meeting place of revolutionaries and intellectuals. Benjamin Franklin, Lafayette and Jefferson all came here. Further along

DISTANCE 1.8 miles (3km)

ALLOW 2.5 hours

START St-Michel Métro station

FINISH Cluny Sorbonne Métro station

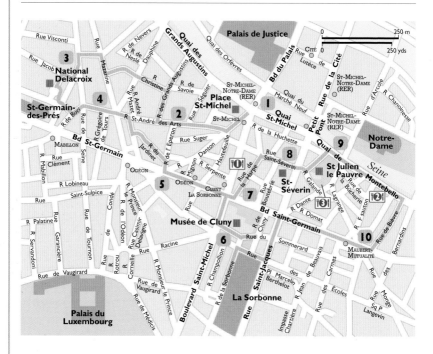

the passageway is the workshop where Dr Guillotine invented 'the nation's razor'. It is said that he practised the blade's action on newborn lambs. During the Revolution some 3,000 people were guillotined. The little courtyard to the left was used during the filming of the musical film *Gigi,* starring Lesley Caron and Maurice Chevalier. In the window of the boutique at the courtyard entrance you can see the remains of a huge stone tower, which was part of the original city wall and dates from the 1180s.

5 Continue through the series of courtyards until you come out on rue du Jardinet. Turn right into rue de l'Eperon, then left along boulevard St-Germain until you reach boulevard St-Michel. Cross over and walk up the boulevard to view the exterior courtyard of the Roman Baths.

The remains of the baths are extensive and date back to the 3rd century. There were three bath complexes in Roman Paris, serving a population of about

20,000, each divided into hot, tepid and cold bathing rooms. The courtyard you are looking into was the tepidarium and the massive paving stones on the floor originally formed the road surface of the Roman rue St-Jacques. Continue around to the rue du Sommerard side, where the corner chamber or steam room can be seen, and huge sections of the collapsed vault lie on the ground. The lower walls of stone and layered brick are still plastered with the original Roman mortar. The ancients used their public baths much as we might use a sauna; here they washed, shaved and came to enjoy aromatherapy massages. Men and women came on separate days.

6 Continue along rue du Sommerard to the entrance of the Musée de Cluny, a little further along on the place Paul Painlevé.

The museum houses an exceptional collection of medieval art and artefacts. The house is late 15th century, a rare example of domestic architecture in the Gothic style. Many churches have survived but there are only three houses from this period in Paris. The courtyard is decorated with carved cockleshells, the emblem of Jacques d'Amboise, for whom the house was built, and holds a curious Wild Man well. The octagonal tower hides a spiral staircase. The striped wall to the left, behind the arcades, is part of the Roman baths, onto which the Cluny mansion was built. One of the most beautiful exhibits here is the series of tapestries known as *The Lady and the*

Unicorn. Scholars still debate the exact meaning of the strange allegories; five of the scenes are known to symbolize the five senses, but the sixth part of the puzzle is not yet fully understood. Other exhibits include stained-glass windows, medieval metalwork, carvings and sculptures, locks and keys, armour, pilgrims' badges and medieval flea combs. There is an excellent book and gift shop. **MUSÉE DE CLUNY;** WED–MON 9.15–5.45; TEL: 01 53 73 78 00; www.musee-moyenage.fr

7 Return to boulevard St-Germain and cross over to rue de la Harpe, by the entrance to Cluny La Sorbonne Métro station. Take rue St-Séverin on the right and go into the church.

The portal is 13th century and was brought here from the Île de la Cité in the 1840s. Most of the building is 15th century, in the style called Flamboyant Gothic. This name comes from the flame shapes in the tracery, as seen in the rose window. Students of the Sorbonne used the church, and the side chapels are decorated with plaques giving thanks for good exam results. At the back of the church are some modern stained glass windows and an ancient well.

8 Continue along rue St-Séverin, cross rue St-Jacques and turn left into rue St-Julien le Pauvre. Stop for a while in front of the church.

Masonry remaining after the completion of Notre-Dame was used to build this lovely old church. The courtyard in front of the building contains a well and just behind it, to the right, is a massive paving stone from the old Roman road. This was the first church of the students at the Sorbonne, and they held elections for the Chancellor of the university here. In the 17th century, students rioted and sacked the church. The first two bays were destroyed and the façade you see today was built to repair it. You can see parts of the ruined original façade on the left-hand side of the courtyard.

9 Cross the garden to quai de Montebello. Turn right. Walk along the quai to rue de Bièvre on your right.

This street is evocative of medieval Paris. Dante stayed here when he began writing his *Inferno* and the infamous Marquise de Brinvilliers, who had a grudge against her family and poisoned several of them, lived at No. 28 for a time (see also Walk 6). No. 22 was the home of President Mitterrand.

10 Turn right into boulevard St-Germain, continue across place Maubert-Mutualité, then turn left into rue St-Jacques and right into rue des Écoles. Stop in front of the statue of Michel de Montaigne.

Michel de Montaigne (1533-1592) was a great thinker of the Renaissance and the father of the essay. He taught here, at the Sorbonne University, which was founded in the 13th century by a monk named Robert de Sorbon. The building you see today dates from the Napoleonic era and was built to educate up to 5,000 students.

By the 1960s, some 20,000 students were crammed in here, a situation that led to the student revolution of May 1968. Nowadays, the university campus comprises some 18 buildings in and around Paris, where 250,000 students are engaged in study. Until the French Revolution, which repressed the university, the language of learning was Latin, but when Napoleon reopened the school he decreed that classes be taught in modern French. You can walk around the building, taking the rue de la Sorbonne to the façade of the Sorbonne church, which is built in the Jesuit style. Inside is the tomb of Cardinal Richelieu, who was chancellor of the university. The walk ends here, at Cluny La Sorbonne Métro station.

145

Down and Out in Paris

The Mouffetard district, in the Latin Quarter, was home to intellectuals in the 1920s. The lively Mouffetard market injects a village atmosphere.

This quarter takes its name from an ancient word, 'La Mouffe', which described the stench for which the area was known. Originally, it was a village separated from Paris by the 12th-century city wall and by a tributary of the Seine called the Bievre. This river powered the mills of the factories that caused the pollution that had earned 'La Mouffe' its name. The Gobelins tapestry works is the last remaining vestige of this quarter's industrial past. The River Bievre had become an open sewer by the 19th century; it still flows underground through Paris today. In the 1920s, Ernest Hemingway lived in this district; nearby, James Joyce finished writing his scandalous book *Ulysses*. The place de la Contrescarpe was known for its rowdy cafés and cabarets, where writers and artists gathered. George Orwell, who lived here to 'experience squalor', describes the quarter in *Down and Out in Paris and London*. The main street of the village – rue Mouffetard – has a fresh-produce market, where goods are artistically displayed. The street is lined with old-fashioned French restaurants and lively exotic cafés.

| Start at Métro Maubert-Mutualité, cross the square, taking rue des Carmes to the Musée de la Prefecture de Police at 1 bis rue des Carmes.

There has been a market here since medieval times; today it is held three times a week (Tue, Thu and Sat). The square is named after a medieval teacher, Maitre Albert. In the Middle Ages, teachers bellowed from first-floor windows to students sitting on bales of straw below. The 14th-century poet, Francois Villon, describes the lessons, the market, and bodies hanging from the gibbets here blackening in the sun, their eyes being pecked out by crows. The Police Museum traces the history of the service from its origins to the introduction of the latest forensic techniques. Documents and objects evoke the most heinous crimes, from the poisonings by Marquise de Brinvilliers (see Walk 6) to the diamond necklace plot against Marie Antoinette. A section is dedicated to the French Resistance and the Liberation of Paris.

2 Leave the museum and take rue Basses des Carmes. Turn right into rue de la Montagne Ste-Genevieve, stopping at place de la Montagne Ste-Genevieve. The École Polytechnique is to the left.

This square is a crossroads where ancient streets meet. Rue de la Montagne Ste-Genevieve has existed since the 12th century and the ancient houses here are labyrinths of dark corridors and courtyards. The little square was famous for its schools and cabarets, which survived until the Revolution. The École Polytechnique, one of the 'Grandes Écoles', opened here in 1805. The school was based on revolutionary ideas of meritocracy. Once qualified, the students must work for the state for a minimum of seven years. Many French politicians and several presidents have been graduates from the Grandes Écoles. Nowadays the students live in the suburbs, away from the distractions of the Latin Quarter.

3 Continue on up the hill to the Panthéon.

This huge building was originally a church, the result of a vow by Louis XV to re-house the shrine of St Genevieve if he was cured of sickness. The church was completed just as the Revolution began in 1789, and the constituent assembly decided that it should become the National Panthéon, where the Great would be honoured. Mirabeau, Voltaire, Rousseau and Marat were buried here, but Mirabeau was later 'de-pantheonized' as he was considered 'not revolutionary enough'. Having once again become a church during the reign of Napoleon III, it was used as the headquarters of the Commune when Napoleon III went into exile. It became a Panthéon again when Victor Hugo was buried here in 1885. The scientist Foucault hung a pendulum from the dome in 1851 to prove that the earth rotates.

PANTHÉON; DAILY 10–6; TEL: 01 44 32 18 00; www.pantheon.monumentsnationaux.fr

OPPOSITE: A GOBELINS TAPESTRY

DISTANCE 1.5 miles (2.5km)

ALLOW 2 hours

START Maubert-Mutualité Métro station

FINISH Les Gobelins Métro station

4 On the left is the church of St-Étienne-du-Mont.

Admire the façade before going inside. Above the main entrance, a semicircular carving shows the stoning of St Stephen, patron saint of the church, which was consecrated in 1629. St Stephen later became the patron of those who suffer from headaches and migraines. Two large figures fill the niches; on the left is St Etienne, symbolizing martyrdom; and right is St Genevieve, shown as a shepherdess. Once inside, walk along the nave towards the rear. Around the choir is a magnificent roodscreen, a carved lacework of stone forming a screen around the choir. Continue past the screen; in the third chapel on the right, behind the screen, is the reliquary of St Genevieve, said to contain her finger bone. Beside this, the stone sarcophagus from the 3rd century is from her original burial. She defended Paris when Attila and the Huns besieged the city, earning her the role of patron saint of Paris. The stained-glass window above her shrine shows her relics being paraded to invoke protection of the city.

5 Continue to the back of the church, leaving by the small side door at the rear on the right. Turn left along rue Clovis. On the right, in the distance, is a large fragment of the Philip August Wall.

This cross-section of the 12th-century wall is one of several that have survived in Paris. The Louvre was built as a bastion to guard the opening caused by the Seine.

The wall was fortified with imposing turreted towers and an internal wooden walkway enabled soldiers to circulate while keeping a lookout for attempts to take the city by invaders.

6 Take the first right turn into rue du Cardinal Lemoine, stopping at No. 74. Ernest Hemingway lived here in a small flat. Continue on to the place de la Contrescarpe.

Hemingway moved into the Mouffetard quarter in 1921 and spent about seven years living in Paris. He describes his flat in his book of memoirs *A Moveable Feast*. The dwelling was very basic, with just two rooms, no hot water and no toilet; he writes of using a bucket, which he would take out to the horse-drawn slops wagon. Hadley, his wife, would go down to get milk from a goat herder who blew a trumpet to announce his arrival. The quarter and the place de la Contrescarpe were famous for their seedy cafés and bars, and several authors of the period have left descriptions of the dirt, drunkenness and endless fights that took place here. Every Friday night a writers' party was organized in the cabaret beneath Hemingway's flat. The novelist Jean Rhys (1890-1979) came here and wrote of the 'sour smell of drunken bodies' and the 'dangerously cheap brandy'. The name of the square comes from the word meaning escarpment, which was a military embankment built up against the exterior of the old city wall. Cafés, bakeries and ice-cream parlours surround the square.

7 Cross the square diagonally, taking rue Mouffetard on the left, then rue du Pot de Fer on the right.

On the corner of the street is one of the seven fountains that once provided the Left Bank with fresh drinking water. These fountains were built as extensions of Marie de Medici's aqueduct, constructed to bring water to the fountains of her Luxembourg Palace gardens. The name Pot de Fer means iron pot, referring to the water carriers' buckets. George Orwell (1903-1950) lived at No. 6 while writing *Down and Out in Paris and London*. He describes the street and its filthy hotels of his time as squalid, although the road is now pleasant, and lined with small restaurants and bistros.

8 Turn left into rue Tournefort, cross onto rue Lhomond and turn into passage des Postes. Turn right back onto rue Mouffetard and walk along to the church of St-Médard on the left.

This end of Mouffetard is the most charming; the market is always busy and the shop fronts are a mixture of ancient architecture. Admire the façades for their old-fashioned shop signs, especially No. 122, 'A la Bonne Source'. This ancient street at one time linked Roman Paris to Rome. The church of St-Médard is largely 16th century and is named after the patron saint of umbrella makers: Médard was once protected from a violent rainstorm when an eagle hovered over him, sheltering him under its spread

WHERE TO EAT

[ⓘ] AUX CERISES DE LUTECE,
86 rue Monge;
Tel: 01 43 31 67 51.
Tearoom and antique shop.

[ⓘ] BISTRO DE LA MONTAGNE,
38 rue de la Montagne Ste-Genevieve;
Tel: 01 43 54 79 68.
Lively and inexpensive, food served in a 13th-century cellar.

[ⓘ] LE BALZAR,
49 rue des Écoles;
Tel: 01 43 54 13 67.
Charming traditional brasserie.

wings. In the 18th century, miraculous cures were said to have taken place in the cemetery here, and soon people were coming from all over to witness the events. The groups that gathered were called the 'Convulsionists' and they had visions, trances, and convulsions that ended in mass hysteria. The cemetery had to be walled up to put an end to the clandestine meetings, and a sign was erected saying 'The King forbids God to perform miracles here'.

9 End the walk by going back to Cardinal Lemoine Métro station. Alternatively, you could continue along the avenue des Gobelins to No. 42, the Manufacture des Gobelins. This is open for guided visits, but these take place in French only. Les Gobelins Métro station is in front of the workshops.

Old-World Forgotten Paris

The sleepy part of Paris near the Jardin des Plantes is locked in the past. Meander through gardens and squares unlike anywhere else in the city.

This quarter has grown up around Paris's Muséum National d'Histoire Naturelle. Its main collections, recently restored, are displayed chronologically in the 'Galerie de l'Evolution'. There is an excellent bookshop, which can be visited without going into the museum. Palaeontology, botany and mineralogy are in separate pavilions along the south side of the garden. The Ménagerie, with reptiles, birds, small mammals and big cats, is fascinating (admission charge). The oldest zoo in France, it was created when the royal menagerie was brought here from Versailles at the time of the Revolution, allowing Parisians to marvel at wild animals such as bears, elephants and giraffes for the first time. However, during the siege of Paris in the 1870s, starving Parisians ate these animals. There is a large Islamic community in this quarter and the Paris Mosque is open for tea and patisseries. The Institute of the Arab World is also here; its rooftop tearoom affords exceptional views, taking in the Seine and Notre-Dame.

I Start at Gare d'Austerlitz Métro
station and walk north along
boulevard de l'Hôpital to place
Valhubert. Cross onto Pont d'Austerlitz
to admire the views, then turn back to
enter the main entrance to the Jardin
des Plantes.

The botanical garden of Paris was
originally a medicinal garden for Louis
XIII. In 1626, two of the king's physicians
obtained permission to establish the
garden; the school of botany, natural
history and pharmacy followed later. As
you enter, the museum buildings and
formal gardens are to the left, and the
Ménagerie, hothouses and Alpine garden
to the right. There is a small maze at the
far right-hand end, near the garden exit
on rue Geoffroy St-Hilaire. The statue
of Jean-Bapitiste Lamarck (1744–1829)
at the entrance commemorates the
18th-century botanist, whose ideas on
evolution were disputed until taken up
again by Darwin in the 19th century.
Admire the façade of the zoology
building, directly ahead. This contains
more than two million pickled, stuffed
or dried animals. Many extinct species,
including the dodo, can be seen here.
The hothouses are masterpieces of
metallic architecture and engineering,
although they had to be restored after the
bombardments of the Franco-Prussian
war of 1871. The tropical gardens within
are well worth visiting.

**MUSÉUM NATIONAL D'HISTOIRE
NATURELLE; MUSÉE DE MINÉRALOGIE;**

WED–MON 10–5; TEL: 01 40 79 56 01;
www.mnhn.fr

2 Leave the garden by the gate
between the Musée de Minéralogie
and the Grande Galerie de l'Évolution.
Opposite is the entrance to La Mosquée.

The Paris Mosque gives an exotic
flavour to this quarter. The large white
building, with its impressive minaret,
was built between 1922 and 1926 in the
Hispano-Moorish style. The large patio
at the centre of the complex was inspired
by the Alhambra Palace in Granada,
Spain. Muslim techniques and crafts
have been used to decorate the building.
The *muezzin* or cantor calls the faithful
to prayer from the 100-ft (33-m) high
minaret. The *Hammam* (Turkish baths) is
open to the public, and there is a separate
boutique selling pieces of Muslim
craftwork. In the tea garden you can sit
under parasols drinking mint tea and
eating traditional pastries.

LA MOSQUÉÉ;

WED–MON 10–5. LA MOSQUÉÉ,
TEL: 01 45 35 97 33; www.la-mosquee.com

DISTANCE **1.5 miles (2.5km)**

ALLOW **2 hours**

START **Gare d'Austerlitz**

FINISH **Cardinale Lemoine Métro station**

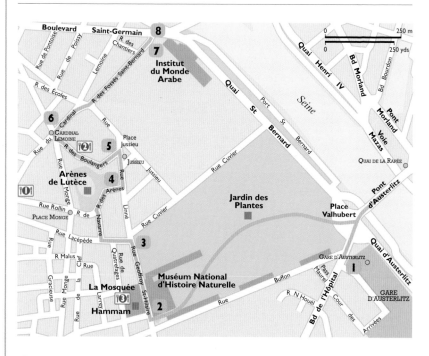

3 Walk along rue Geoffroy St-Hilaire, turning left into rue Lacepède, then right into rue Navarre. Opposite is the entrance to the Arènes de Lutèce.

About two-thirds of the original structure of this spectacular Roman arena has survived. Until the mid-19th century, when archaeologists became interested in the city's Roman past, the arena was hidden under a mass of buildings and the central ring had become a bus depot. Explore the paths that climb the rows

of seating, now only two-thirds their original height. The arena was used for blood sports and could seat about 20,000 spectators, which was more or less the total population of Roman Paris. It could be flooded with water from the nearby River Bievre; water ducts can be seen in front of the stage. The cage doors in the side of the arena were used for releasing dangerous animals during gladiator fights. The main entrance, through which the crowds poured for performances, was referred to as the vomitorium. Traces of

WHERE TO EAT

ĪŌĪ L'EPOQUE,
81 rue du Cardinal Lemoine;
Tel: 01 46 34 15 84.
Old-style bistro.

ĪŌĪ MAYJU,
36 rue des Boulangers;
Tel: 01 44 07 13 29.
Dishes from around the world.

ĪŌĪ THE MOSQUE,
39 rue Geoffroy St-Hilaire;
Tel: 01 43 31 38 20.
Tearoom and patisserie/couscous.

post-holes have been found, confirming that the arena could be covered with canvas to protect spectators from the heat in summer or the rain in winter. The stage wall was originally much higher and the small chambers behind it were changing rooms for performers.

4 Go into the Capitan square on the right and leave by the exit on rue des Arènes. Turn left into rue Linné, stopping at place Jussieu.

During term-time about 10,000 students a day study at this university complex. The buildings date from the 1960s and are barrack-like and unimaginative. The university complex is divided into rigid square courtyards with a massive tower in the centre. There is as much charm here as in the average multi-storey carpark, although in the 1980s various famous

artists set about decorating the courtyards with modern works, especially around the faculty of sciences named after Pierre and Marie Curie. Along rue Jussieu there is a small museum where the department of Minéralogie displays some of its most spectacular gems. The number of students in the area ensures a lively and dynamic atmosphere and ensures that the prices in the cafés, snack bars and bookshops remain affordable.

5 Take rue des Boulangers, on the opposite side of the square, and walk along to Cardinal Lemoine Métro station.

This steep and winding street dates back to the 14th century. Many of the houses here are ancient, with charming details such as dormer windows, ironwork balustrades and large ornate portals. The road is named after the bakers who settled here in large numbers in the 16th century. Houses 19–31 are built on the site of a convent for English girls. Aurore Dupin, who became a famous French novelist under the pen name of George Sand (1804-1876), was educated here.

6 At Cardinal Lemoine Métro station turn right and head downhill on rue du Cardinal Lemoine towards the Seine. Fork right and continue along rue des Fossés Saint-Bernard.

At No. 49 rue du Cardinal Lemoine stop to admire the lovely Le Brun town house built in 1700 for a nephew of the celebrated painter Charles Le Brun,

who was in charge of the decorative scheme at Versailles. For a while it was home to the painter Watteau, then in the 1760s Buffon, Natural Historian of the botanical gardens, lived here. It is the most magnificent residence in the quarter, built by the architect Germain Boffrand (1667-1754) using the Roman architect Vitruvius's architectural formula as set out in his work *De Architectura*.

7 Continue to the Institut du Monde Arab at 23 quai St-Bernard.

The IMA (Arab World Institute) was founded in the 1980s as a joint project with France and 19 Arab countries. The idea was to build a cultural centre and museum that would promote harmony between French and Arabic cultures, although squabbles about who would pay for what led to several years of delay

and disharmony. The architect whose plans were chosen was Jean Nouvel (b. 1945), the man responsible for many of Paris's modern buildings. There is a library here, with only one shelf that spirals continually up the five floors of the documentation centre. The southern façade of the building consists of light-sensitive screens modelled on the carved wooden screens called *moucharabiehs* used in buildings from Morocco to southeast Asia. The screens are computer-controlled so that the openings increase or reduce in size, depending on the amount of daylight. The screens can be seen at close quarters if you go in, and it is highly recommended that you take the lift to the seventh-storey tearoom to enjoy the spectacular views across the city.

8 The walk ends here. Return to Cardinal Lemoine Métro station.

Down Among the Bones

Beneath the streets of Paris is one of the strangest museums in the world, Les Catacombes. This walk is not for the claustrophobic.

The Denfert quarter of Paris is quiet and peaceful, a predominantly residential quarter with a lovely fresh produce market along the rue Daguerre. The area was countrified until the 19th century and is home to many convents and monasteries. The Observatory is located here as well as the elegant building that houses the hospital 'Val de Grace'. It is hard to imagine that 65ft (20m) beneath your feet is a museum, where you can walk through nearly 0.6 miles (1km) of underground passageways, cut by human hand into the bedrock of Paris. These subterranean corridors are embossed with the bones of six million Parisians who lived between the medieval period and the 18th century. One cannot help but contemplate mortality here, for this underground cemetery is a harsh reminder of the inevitability of death and perfectly illustrates Shelley's poem *Death the Leveller*, which states that in death we are all the same. Nineteenth-century visitors were given a candle and followed a black line painted on the ceiling. Today, a pocket torch is useful for shining into the nooks and crannies.

Start the walk at Denfert-Rochereau Métro station.

The square is named after a colonel who, along with a group of brave soldiers, defended the town of Belfort during the wars of 1870. The bronze lion is a reduced-size copy of the Lion at Belfort, which symbolizes the colonel's heroic defence. It was made by Bartholdi, sculptor of the Statue of Liberty. Either side of the square are two pavilions; originally these were the toll booths controlling the Denfert gateway into the 18th-century walled city of Paris. Nowadays, the one on the Métro side is administrative offices for the quarry services, while the one on the left is the entrance to Les Catacombes. Stop in the lobby of the building, beside the entrance, to see fascinating models of the quarries.

LES CATACOMBES;

TUE–SUN 10–4 (Closed public holidays)
TEL: 01 43 22 47 63;

2 Purchase a ticket or use the museum pass. After the turnstile, begin your downward climb (90 steps), then follow the underground corridor until you come to the chamber called the Atelier.

Clandestine meetings have been organized in this chamber since the 18th century, when covens of witches, smugglers and secret societies all used the chamber to conduct their nefarious business. During World War II, members of the French Resistance established their headquarters here. The first part of the tunnel consists of stone walls built to support the quarry roof; the second part, curiously coffin-shaped, is hewn directly into the stone. The Atelier is part of the quarry. As you arrive, look down a corridor that has been closed off by a collapse. You can see where banks of stone have been cut out. Women and children were employed to push carts filled with the stone to the quarry exits. As the stone was removed, apple core-shaped pillars were left to support the quarry roof. A quarry worker called Ducure was killed here in a collapse, and the thin veins of red iron ore that seep through the stone walls were said to be his blood. During the Revolution, a porter from the nearby hospital decided to explore the tunnel; he got lost and his body was eventually found 11 years later. He was identified by his bunch of keys.

3 Continue along to the entrance of the bone depository (ossuary).

Above the entrance is the inscription 'Stop. Here lies the empire of death!' It is estimated that the bones of six million Parisians lie here. The majority come from the cemetery of the Innocents, but bones from many other churchyards were brought here during the 18th century. There were several direct burials during the Revolution, when the victims of massacres were brutally thrown down here and left to rot. Originally, the bones were simply stacked in piles. Napoleon's government had the bones arranged into the patterns and mosaics that line the corridors today.

OPPOSITE: LES CATACOMBES

23

DISTANCE 1.5 miles (2.5km)

ALLOW 2.5 hours

START Denfert-Rochereau Métro station

FINISH Port Royal Métro station

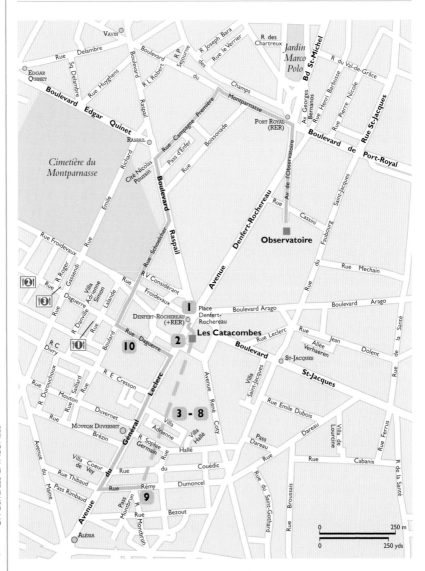

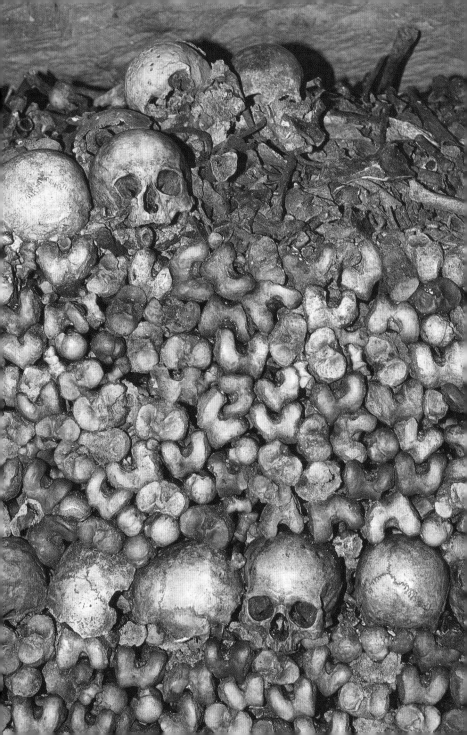

4 From the ossuary, continue to the Fontaine de la Samaritaine (well chamber), and then to the Crypt du Sacellum.

This well, built to provide drinking water for the quarry workers, was nicknamed the 'footbath', as the workers could not see it in the dark and consequently regularly stepped in it. The name Samaritaine refers to the Samarian woman who offered water to Christ. The Crypt du Sacellum was used as a church; regular masses were held here, and on 2 April 1897, it was the scene of a clandestine midnight concert. On the programme were Saint Saens's *Danse Macabre* and various funeral marches. The quarry staff responsible for admitting the orchestra and guests were later sacked. Marie Antoinette's friend, Mme de Polignac, held a banquet here, and the Comte d'Artois, who later became King Charles X, organized secret dinners. Parisians still find illicit ways to enter at night and empty champagne bottles can often be seen behind the stacks of bones.

5 The circuit then takes you to a small monument called La Lampe Sépucrale (the Sepulchral Lamp), then on to Tombeau dit 'de Gilbert' (The Tomb of Gilbert).

This small monument was the first to be put up in Les Catacombes. Originally, a brazier was kept alight here because the fire improved the circulation of air. The tomb is simply a monument; there is no body here. The unfortunate poet Gilbert (1751–1780), wrote a moving verse about death in 1780. Eight days later he died after falling from his horse.

6 Keep walking until you come to a sharp U-turn.

The two stone monuments here commemorate victims of the Revolution. The ongoing fighting in Paris led to dreadful massacres in August 1788, when the Finance Minister, Brienne, resigned, and on 28 April 1789, when factory workers revolted. In 1792, hysterical Parisians rampaged through the prisons of the city, killing innocent and guilty alike. On 10 August 1792, some 2,000 were killed when the Sans Culottes group of Revolutionaries threatened to storm the Tuileries Palace unless the king was deposed. Their bones lie here.

7 Continue towards the exit. In a small chapel of bones on the left are the remains brought from the Madeleine cemetery.

This cemetery was near the place de la Concorde, where the guillotine was located. The remains of those who were decapitated were unceremoniously cast into a communal grave. The bones were later brought here and probably include those of historical figures such as Danton, Robespierre, Mme Roland, and maybe even Marie Antoinette and Louis XVI.

8 Follow the quarry inspection tunnel (galleries maçonées et appareillées) to the exit.

The last leg of the journey (no pun intended) is fascinating. Keep looking up: you will walk beneath two massive bell-shaped chambers. These seemingly suspended cone shapes are the results of subsidence. They are extremely dangerous, because as a dome of rock detaches itself in this bell shape it is not detectable from the surface; if a vehicle passes over the remaining thin surface layer it can suddenly find itself 100ft (30m) underground. The last serious collapse took place in December 1995 in the 9th district of Paris. As you exit Les Catacombes, be prepared for a bag check; in this museum they are more worried about what you might take out rather than what you may bring in with you.

9 Exit on the rue Rémy Dumoncel and turn right to avenue Générale Leclerc. Turn right, continuing on the left-hand side until rue Daguerre.

This road is a pleasant market street filled with cafés, local restaurants and fresh food stalls. It is lively and picturesque and makes a good lunch stop, especially after the darkness of Les Catacombes. The road is named after Daguerre, the French inventor of photography.

10 Walk along rue Daguerre, turn right into rue Boulard, then continue straight on into rue Schœlcher. Turn left into boulevard Raspail, right into rue Campagne Première and right along boulevard du Montparnasse, stopping at the corner of avenue de l'Observatoire.

WHERE TO EAT

🍽 AU BISTROT,
18 rue Lalande;
Tel: 01 43 20 00 28.
Local traditional restaurant.

🍽 LE BISTROT DES PINGOUINS,
79 rue Daguerre;
Tel: 01 43 21 92 29.
Contemporary French cuisine.

🍽 AUX PETITS CHANDELIERS,
62 rue Daguerre;
Tel: 01 43 20 25 87.
Ethnic and Caribbean food.

Construction of the Observatory, situated on the Paris meridian, began on the day of the summer solstice in 1667. London's Greenwich meridian was more or less universally adopted in 1884, but Paris continued to use its own until 1911. The speed of light was calculated here, and in 1679 the Observatory produced a detailed map of the moon. In 1846, Le Verrier (1811–1877) proved the existence of Neptune here by mathematical deduction. Today, the Observatory is still an important scientific research centre, and the oldest functioning building of its type in the world. The world's first speaking clock was set up here in 1933. On the far side of the boulevard are the Luxembourg gardens, an ideal picnic lunch spot. The nearest Métro station is Port Royal, but you can end your walk opposite at the Closerie des Lilas, a café frequented by Ernest Hemingway.

Painters' Paris

Follow the footsteps of 19th-century artists such as Picasso, Matisse and Modigliani, who came to Montparnasse to be near the Paris Art School.

Once open fields, Montparnasse was the place where students from the university came to find inspiration from the muses of Mount Parnassus. As the area was not built up, artists and sculptors could rent small cottages with gardens quite cheaply, and at the turn of the 20th century, Paris was the place to be; many artists fled here to escape anti-Jewish pogroms and persecution in Eastern Europe. The combination of cheap food and accommodation, inspiring teachers and all-night cafés attracted Picasso, Matisse, Modigliani, Soutine and Chagall. During the Occupation, when the Métro was the only means of transport, the local station was closed down. St-Germain-des-Prés remained open, so the café clients migrated south, and that became the area for evening entertainment. Brutal redevelopment in the 1960s left a scar on this neighbourhood, but there are still some quaint back streets to enjoy. As the station links Brittany to Paris, many local streets are lined with restaurants serving traditional Breton crêpes and galettes. These delicacies are inexpensive, informal and tasty.

1 Exit Montparnasse Bienvenüe Métro station (exit No. 2). Walk down avenue du Maine and go to the Musée du Montparnasse at No. 21.

A charming enclave of creeper-covered artists' studios houses the small-scale Montparnasse Museum. It's in the building where the Russian painter Marie Vassilieff (1884-1957) operated an informal free canteen for her poor artist friends during World War I. In the evenings, they amused themselves in a homespun way: Modigliani sang, Marie Vassilieff performed Russian folk dances, and Picasso mimicked them. The museum specializes in exhibitions of artwork from the 1920s, the era for which this district is most famous.

MUSÉE DU MONTPARNASSE;
WED–SUN 1–7; TEL: 01 42 22 91 96;
www.museums-of-paris.com

2 Leave the museum, turn left into avenue du Maine and head for the modern skyscraper, Tour Montparnasse.

The Montparnasse Tower, which provides office space, was built in the late 1960s and is two-thirds the height of the Eiffel Tower. The view is spectacular from the 56th floor and, unlike the Eiffel Tower, the lift to the top is very speedy (you will probably leave your stomach at the bottom). If you crave a view of the rooftops of Paris but do not want to wait in line at the Eiffel Tower, it provides a good alternative. No one knows how permission was gained to build the tower as, in theory, there is a height limit on the buildings in Paris. Allegedly, the then Minister of Culture was given a bribe.

TOUR MONTPARNASSE;
DAILY 9.30–11.30; TEL: 01 45 38 52 56;
www.tourmontparnasse56.com

3 Cross rue du Départ and go ahead into boulevard Edgar Quinet. On the left you will pass rue d'Odessa and rue du Montparnasse, lined with inexpensive and lively crêperies, the Breton speciality for which the district is well known. Continue along boulevard Edgar Quinet until you reach the Cimetière du Montparnasse at No. 3.

This large cemetery, originally established outside the city limits, has many famous tombs. Pick up a free plan from the office on the left as you enter; it will help you find the graves of Jean-Paul Sartre, Simone de Beauvoir, Samuel Beckett, and Charles Garnier, who designed the Opera House. There are also some elaborate, poignant and extraordinary tombs. Look

169

DISTANCE **1.2 miles (2km)**

ALLOW **2 hours**

START **Montparnasse Bienvenüe Métro station**

FINISH **Port Royal Métro station**

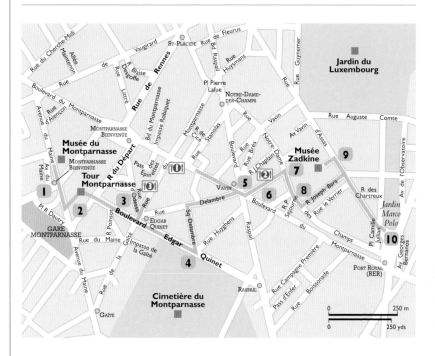

out for the tomb of the Pigeon family, depicting a couple in bed (fully dressed).

4 Exit the cemetery where you came in. Cross boulevard Edgar Quinet and go through square Delambre, ahead. Turn right into rue Delambre and walk to No. 9, where the dancer Isadora Duncan lived, and No. 10, the Dingo Bar where Hemingway drank with Scott-Fitzgerald. At the end of the road, turn left. Boulevard du Montparnasse is lined with restaurants and brasseries.

These famous eating places were particularly popular in the early 20th century, when the area was a Mecca for artists and writers and the cafés stayed open until very late. People left the clubs, which closed in the early hours of the morning, and found an all-night café where they could have an early breakfast. The most unchanged establishments are La Coupole at No. 102, with its attractive wall paintings by the needy artists of the day – they say the 30 artists whose work can be seen represents the number who

OPPOSITE: TOMB OF THE PIGEON FAMILY

could not pay their bills – and opposite, at No. 99, the Select Bar. Here Hemingway set much of his novel *The Sun Also Rises*.

5 Retrace your steps to the junction of boulevard du Montparnasse and boulevard Raspail, where Rodin's statue of Balzac is in the middle of the road.

This statue, made originally in the 1890s, was shocking in its day. People expected the writer Balzac to be in a top hat and frock coat, but Rodin captured the strength of his novels and the essence of his personality by a huge, simple figure reminiscent of a powerful standing stone.

6 Cross boulevard Raspail and take the first left into rue de la Grande Chaumière.

On this street there are several art schools that date back to the early 20th century. Students still come here from all over the world to study art. Peep into any of the

courtyards – you will see they are lined with artists' studios. No. 9 is the hotel where Samuel Beckett stayed; Gauguin, Mucha and Modigliani all used the studios at No. 8.

7 Turn right at the end of rue de la Grande Chaumière into rue Notre-Dame des Champs and continue to No. 86 with its wall of artists' studios.

The American-born artist James Whistler (1834-1903) lived here for many years. His most famous painting, *Arrangement in Grey and Black: Portrait of the Painter's Mother* (otherwise known as *Whistler's Mother*) can be seen in Paris in the Musée d'Orsay. He had planned to paint a nude but the model didn't show up, so he asked his mother to sit for him instead. His works were often considered too modern because people felt they didn't tell a story, but he said a painting could be like music, which is why he gave his works titles such as 'Arrangement' or

'Harmony'. Hemingway lived further up this street, above a saw mill, at No. 113, but the building no longer stands.

8 Turn left down rue Joseph Bara, and go left again into rue d'Assas. Walk to No. 100 and into the courtyard of the Musée Zadkine.

Even if you do not wish to go inside this museum, do venture into the courtyard. Here you will see an example of the many small houses set in gardens that made the area so popular with artists. Sculptors, in particular, needed ground-floor accommodation to house their heavy materials. Zadkine (1890-1967) was a Russian artist who fled to France to escape anti-Semitism. One of his most expressive sculptures, which you can see in the garden, is a figure with its arms raised in a gesture of despair and protest. Seen as the sculptural version of Picasso's *Guernica,* it was made to commemorate the bombing of Rotterdam by the Nazis.

MUSEE ZADKINE;

TUE–SUN 10–6; TEL: 01 55 42 77 20; www.paris.fr/portail/Culture/Portal.lut

9 As you exit the museum turn right into rue d'Assas. Walk to the end to the Closerie des Lilas.

Now rather pricey, this restaurant was Hemingway's favourite place to write. He liked it because it was full of unpretentious French people, not foreigners posing as writers who would interrupt his creative flow for a chat. In front of the restaurant is a statue of

WHERE TO EAT

🍽 LA COUPOLE,
102 boulevard du Montparnasse;
Tel: 01 43 20 14 20.
Large, lively traditional brasserie.

🍽 WAJDA,
10 rue de la Grande chaumiere;
Tel: 01 46 33 02 02.
Small bistro.

🍽 LE BIGOUDEN,
62 rue du Montparnasse;
Tel: 01 43 20 24 85.
Breton crèperie.

Marshall Ney, a Napoleonic general whose execution was ordered on this spot after Waterloo. It is claimed that the execution was a sham, as the soldiers did not want to execute one of their own generals. He is said to have escaped and ended his life in America.

10 Cross rue d'Assas and head towards a large statue in the centre of a fountain, surrounded by horses, at the entrance to the Jardin du Luxembourg.

This beautiful sculpture by Jean-Baptiste Carpeaux (1827-1875), symbolizes the Four Corners of the World; four women from different continents are represented. The horses and turtles who seem to cavort in the water jets are particularly attractive. The walk ends here. Port Royal Métro station is behind you.

INDEX

Abbesses, place des 83
Alexander III Bridge 107, 114–16
Angelina's tearoom 75
l'Arbre Sec, rue de 23
Arc de Carrousel 15–16
Arc de Triomphe 15, 98, 99, 103
Les Archives Nationales 39–40
Arènes de Lutèce 156–8
'Au Pied de Cochon' 25

Bakers' Corporation 65–6
Balzac, Honoré de 60, 172
Barrio Latino 54
Bastille 36, 42, 50–5, 65, 107
Beaubourg 28–33
Beaumarchais, Pierre-Augustin
    de 39, 52
Bievre, rue de 145
Les Billettes 43
Boulangers, rue des 158
La Bourse du Commerce 22, 23
Bourse des Valeurs 26
Brinvilliers, Marquise de 47

Callas, Maria 61
canal St Martin 51
Canettes, rue des 138
Capucines, boulevard des 96–7
Carpeaux, Jean-Baptiste 173
Castel Beranger 127–8, 130
Les Catacombes 32, 162, 163–7
Catherine de Medici 15, 23, 85,
    99
Centre Pompidou 28, 32–3
Champs-Elysées 98, 99–100, 103
Chantier, passage du 54–5
Chapelle Expiatoire 71
Charles V, King 42, 46, 50
Charles IX, King 18
Charles X, King 166
Châtelet 29
Cimetière du Montparnasse
    169–70

Cimetière de Passy 121
Cimetière du Père-Lachaise
    56–61
Cler, rue 124
Closerie des Lilas 173
Conciergerie 9, 29
Concorde, place de la 99, 107,
    166
Contrescarpe, place de la 152
La Coupole 170–2
Cour d'Honneur 113–14, 124
Cour du Commerce St-André
    141–2
Crypt du Sacellum 166
Crypte Archaeologique 10
Curie, Marie 68

The Da Vinci Code 16, 18, 136,
    139
Daguerre, rue 167
La Défense 98, 103
Dehillerin 23–5
Delacroix, Eugène 60, 136, 141
Denfert quarter 162–7
Dr Blanche, square du 131
Dreyfus, Captain 124
Duca, Cino del 58

Ecole de Médecine 139
Ecole Militaire 122–4
Ecole Polytechnique 149
Les Égouts 117
Eiffel Tower 120–1, 122, 169
Elysée Palace 99–100
Epstein, Jacob 61

Flamel, Nicolas 29, 33
Forum des Halles 25
French Revolution 9, 51, 68, 71,
    99, 114, 142, 145, 163, 166
Furstemberg, place 141

Géricault, Théodore 57–8

Golden Triangle 98, 102–3
Grand Palais 100, 116
La Grande Arche 98, 103
Guimard, Hector 83, 126,
    127–31

Les Halles 22–7
Haussmann, Baron 84, 85, 92
Haussmann, boulevard 93
Hemingway, Ernest 135, 139,
    148, 152, 167, 170, 172, 173
Henri Heine, rue 130–1
Henry II, King 18, 85
Henry IV, King 19, 32, 37, 64
Hermès 74
Hôtel Amelot de Bisseuil 39
Hôtel Chenizot 68
Hôtel Dieu 10
Hôtel Lambert 65
Hôtel de Lauzun 66
Hôtel Matignon 112
Hôtel Meurice 97
Hôtel Mezzara 130
Hôtel de Sens 46
Hôtel de Ville 43, 68
Hugo, Victor 13, 28, 30, 37, 47,
    149

Île de la Cité 8–13, 43, 140
Île St-Louis 64–9
Innocents, place des 32
Institut du Monde Arabe 154,
    159
Intercontinental Le Grand Hôtel
    96
Les Invalides 97, 98, 100, 112,
    113–14

Jardin du Luxembourg 135, 153,
    167, 173
Jardin des Plantes 155
Jardins du Trocadéro 120, 121
Jardin des Tuileries 15, 99, 110

Jasmin, square 130
Jeu de Paume 99
Joan of Arc, St 15, 71, 74, 79
Jouffroy, passage 26
Jussieu, place 158

Knights Templar 9, 40

Lapin Agile 82
Lappe, rue de 52–4
Latin Quarter 134–9, 140–5,
    148–53
Le Corbusier 126, 131
Louis IX, King (St Louis) 9, 55, 79
Louis XI, King 50, 54–5
Louis XIII, King 18, 37, 47, 155
Louis XIV, King 19, 25, 37, 40, 42,
    50, 97, 100, 112, 126
Louis XV, King 149
Louis XVI, King 39, 70, 71, 99,
    166
Louis XVI, square 71
Louis XVII, King 40
Louvre 14, 16–18, 20–1, 110,
    152
Luxembourg Palace 135

La Madeleine 70, 74, 107
Madeleine district 70–5
La Madeleine, place de la 74
Maison de Radio France 127
Mallet-Stevens, Robert 126, 131
Marais 36–41, 42–7
Marché Ste Catherine, place du
    37
Marché St Germain 138–9
Marie Antoinette, Queen
    9, 23, 40, 55, 70, 71, 99, 138,
    149, 166
Marie de Medici 135, 153
Maupassant, Guy de 85
Mémorial de la Déportation
    8, 13, 46
Ménagerie 154, 155
Menier Mansion 89
Monceau quarter 84–9

Mont de Pieté 39, 40
Montagne St-Genevieve, place
    de la 149
Montaigne, Michel de 145
Montmartre 78–83
Montorgueil, rue 26
Montparnasse 168–73
Mouffetard district 148–53
Moulin de la Galette 83
Moulin Rouge 83, 90–1
Musée des Arts et Métiers 28,
    33
Musée Carnavalet 37
Musée Cernuschi 85–6
Musée de Cluny 144
Musée Fragonard 96
Musée Grévin 26
Musée Jacquemart André 88–9
Musée de la Légion d'Honneur
    109
Musée Marmottan 127
Musée de Minéralogie 155
Musée du Montmartre 82
Musée du Montparnasse 169
Musée National d'Art Moderne
    33
Musée Nissim de Camondo
    86–8
Musée d'Orsay 109–10
Musée Picasso 40
Musée Rodin 113
Musée Zadkine 173
Muséum National d'Histoire
    Naturelle 154, 155

Napoleon I, Emperor
    9, 15–16, 29, 70, 74, 96, 97, 98,
    100, 103, 113, 114, 121, 122,
    124, 139, 145
Napoleon III, Emperor 71, 84, 92,
    93, 96, 149
National Assembly (Assemblée
    Nationale) 70, 107, 108
Notre-Dame 8, 11–13, 33, 67
Notre-Dame de la Consolation
    102

Observatory 167
Odéon, rue de l' 139
Olympia 97
Opéra Bastille 51
Opéra district 92–7
Opéra Garnier 92, 93–6
Orangerie 99

Palais Bourbon, place du 108
Palais de Chaillot 121, 122
Palais de la Découverte 100–2
Palais Royal 14, 19
Panoramas, passage des 26
Panthéon 149
Parc du Champ de Mars 122–4
Paris Mosque 154, 155
Petit Palais 100, 116
Philip August Wall 152
Picasso, Pablo 40, 78, 82, 89, 140,
    141, 168, 169, 173
Police Museum 149
Poncelet, passage 89
Pont de l'Alma 117
Pont des Arts 110
Pont de la Concorde 107
Pont d'Iéna 122
Pont Neuf 9
Port de Plaisance 51
Pont de Solferino 110
Pont de la Tournelle 68
promenade Plantée 55

Qinze Vingt 55

Rimbaud, Arthur 65
Rocher de Cancale' 26, 27
Rodin, Auguste 109, 113, 130,
    172
Roman Baths 140, 142–4
Rosiers, rue des 39
Rossini, Gioacchino 57

Sacré-Coeur 79
St Alexander Nevsky 89
St Augustin 71
Sainte-Chapelle 9

St Denis 80–2
St-Etienne-du-Mont 152
St Eustache 22, 25
St-Germain-l'Auxerrois 18–19
St Germain des Prés Church
  139
St-Germain-des-Prés quarter
  134–9
St-Gervais 43–4
St-Honoré, rue 74–5
St-Julien le Pauvre 144–5
St-Louis en l'Ile 67
St-Médard 153
St-Merri 29–30
St-Michel, place 141
St Paul 47
St-Pierre 79

St Pierre du Gros Caillou 116
St Pol 42
St-Roch 15
St-Severin 144
St-Sulpice 135–8
Sandrié, Impasse 96
Sebastopol, boulevard 30–2
Seine, River 8, 43, 64, 106, 110
Sevigné, Mme de 37, 47, 74
sewers 117
Sorbonne University 140, 144,
  145
Soubise Palace 40

Temple, square du 40
Tertre, place du 80
Théâtre de l'Odéon 139

Théâtre de la Ville 29
Tour Jean Sans Peur 25–6
Tour Montparnasse 169
Tour St Jacques 28, 29
Trinité church 93

Van Gogh, Vincent 83
Vendôme, place 97
Verdeau, passage 26
Viaduc des Arts 55
Village St-Paul 46–7
Vosges, place des 37

Whistler, James 109, 172–3
Wilde, Oscar 61

Zadkine, Ossip 33, 173

ACKNOWLEDGEMENTS

The Automobile Association would like to thank the following photographers, companies and picture libraries for their assistance in the preparation of this book.

Abbreviations for the picture credits are as follows – (t) top; (b) bottom; (c) centre; (l) left; (r) right; (AA) AA World Travel Library.

3 Directphoto.org/Alamy; 6/7 Lebrecht Music and Arts Photo Library/Alamy; 8 Pictures Colour Library; 11 Pictures Colour Library; 12 Moritz Steiger/Alamy; 14 World Pictures/Photoshot; 17 Pictures Colour Library; 18 AA/J Tims; 19 AA/M Jourdan; 20/21 Pictures Colour Library; 22 AA/C Sawyer; 27 Guichaoua/Alamy; 28 AA/B Rieger; 31 AA/T Souter; 32 AA/M Jourdan; 34/35 Art Kowalsky/Alamy; 36 AA/M Jourdan; 39 AA/C Sawyer; 41 AA/P Kenward; 42 AA/P Kenward; 43 AA/P Kenward; 45 Pictures Colour Library; 46 AA/B Rieger; 48/49 Pictures Colour Library; 50 David A. Barnes/Alamy; 51 Danita Delimont/Alamy; 53 AA/C Sawyer; 54 Directphoto.org/Alamy; 56 AA/M Jourdan; 57 AA/T Souter; 59 Paul Shawcross/Alamy; 61 Pictures Colour Library; 62/63 World Pictures/Photoshot; 64 Pictures Colour Library; 65 Chuck Pefley/Alamy; 67 Christel Broque/Alamy; 69 Rough Guides/Alamy; 70/71 Pictures Colour Library; 72 AA/M Jourdan; 75 Pictures Colour Library; 77 AA/B Rieger; 78 AA/P Enticknap; 79 AA/T Souter; 81 Pictures Colour Library; 82 AA; 84 AA/K Paterson; 87 AA/B Rieger; 88 AA/J Tims; 90/91 Pictures Colour Library; 92 AA/K Paterson; 95 Pictures Colour Library; 97 AA/C Sawyer; 98 AA/K Paterson; 100 images-of-france/Alamy; 102 AA/C Sawyer; 103 AA/P Kenward; 104/105 Pictures Colour Library; 106 World Pictures/Photoshot; 107 tbkmedia.de/Alamy; 111 AA/ P Enticknap; 112 AA/K Paterson; 115 AA/K Paterson; 116 Glyn Thomas/Alamy; 117 Andrew Carruth/Alamy; 118/119 Pictures Colour Library; 120 AA/J Tims; 121 AA/T Souter; 125 AA/T Souter; 126 AA/B Rieger; 129 AA/B Rieger; 131 AA/B Rieger; 132/133 Pictures Colour Library; 134 F1 online/Alamy; 135 AA; 137 Pictures Colour Library; 138 AA/K Paterson; 140 AA/B Rieger; 143 AA/C Sawyer; 145 Kalicoba/Alamy; 146/147 AA/M Jourdan; 148 Visual Arts Library (London)/Alamy; 151 AA/J Tims; 154 Bertrand Collet/Alamy; 155 AA/M Jourdan; 157 PCL/Alamy; 159 AA/M Jourdan; 160/161 Pictures Colour Library; 162 AA/J Tims; 165 AA/K Paterson; 168 Acro Images/Alamy; 169 Rough Guides/Alamy; 171 Chuck Pefley/Alamy; 172 AA/C Sawyer.

Every effort has been made to trace the copyright holders, and we apologise in advance for any accidental errors. We would be happy to apply the corrections in the following edition of this publication.